ARISE addresses the essenc
revealed, will set you on a n
one of thriving in your God-

Reverend Alistair Howie, M.A. –
Lead Corporate Chaplain and Founder of Chaplain 360

We all have a story to tell, but not all of us are brave
enough to tell it. The human experience is naturally
fraught with insecurity, pain, and often sorrow. In ARISE,
Michele Francesca Cohen vulnerably shares her story
as a way to help us who have become so submerged
in our suffering that we have lost our way, or even our
hope. Over the years, I've known Michele in both the
depths of her suffering and in the beauty of her healing.
I've seen her broken and I've seen her restored. She is a
living illustration of the power of a personal relationship
with Christ and its ability to redeem even our most
broken moments. This is why this book is so powerful. I
recommend it to everyone who has ever been lost, lonely,
or weary to the bone. In it you will find the strength and
confidence to trust Christ in greater measure, so that He
might turn your story from loss to victory.

Jan Greenwood –
Author of *Women at War*
Equip Pastor, Gateway Church

As a champion of women in the workplace, I find ARISE is
a must read for every woman. Michele Francesca Cohen
shares her deepest fears and how she moved from living
a minimized existence to living her purpose with passion.
Find your freedom to be the authentic you in the pages
of this book.

Bethany Williams –
International Best-Selling Author of *CEO of You*
CEO of BWE & Host of *3 Days to a Raise*

Terrific style and even better content, ARISE is a compelling book with gripping stories and insightful application that will lead you to a critical intercession of decision.

Peace, courage, and freedom to be the real you without fear is what you'll experience reading Michele Francesca Cohen's book, ARISE. It's a must read for anyone trying to overcome deep-seated fears that hold you back in life.

When James writes, "Count it all joy when you fall into various trials..." most of us scratch our heads and say, "What?" We associate God's favor with an adversity-free life. And yet as Michele Francesca Cohen teaches us in this powerful book, it is in these various trials that the Holy Spirit draws us close and loves us until we ARISE to our best selves.

Hear the holy call to recognize this Kairos moment – to embrace our identity founded in the image of God, just as God's kingdom literally inhabits the earth. ARISE reminds us of the biblical mandate to embrace His-story in each of our lives through authentic, absolute surrender. Be prepared for Michele's story to move and challenge you to arise from your ashes and shine brilliantly, so that, through us, His glory will cover the earth as the waters cover the seas.

In ARISE, you will love both the journey and the destination. Before even finishing chapter three, God healed me of an old soul wound. Fasten your seatbelt because you will see things differently than before; your faith will deepen as your concept of God transforms and the process of arising changes you. Well written, ARISE had me laughing and "leaking tears" in the span of just a few pages. It's not often that one experiences revelation as new and fresh as Michele articulates here. You will never be the same.

Wes Carlton –
Worship Leader, Author, Inventor
CEO of Loss Management Solutions

If you have walked through a hard time, experienced loss, or been in the pit after a tragedy, then ARISE may be exactly what you need to put your feet on solid ground. Sharing from her experience in the pit, Michele Francesca Cohen offers comfort, hope, and reassurance. Allow her testimony to illuminate the way out of darkness to a place of safety. You will be so glad you joined her on this journey with God, from sitting in ashes to brushing them off and arising to her true self. You may find your own true self by the time you finish reading ARISE.

Anne Ashton –
Artist, Speaker, Writer & Activator
www.annerdashton.com

ARISE

Michele Francesca Cohen

ARISE

Copyright © 2017 by Michele Francesca Cohen. All Rights Reserved

By: Michele Francesca Cohen

Edited by Courtney Cohen, Now Found Publishing, LLC.

Photography by Sian and Lindsey Smith, Ashlyn Media

Cover design, Book design, Layout, & Production by Steven Cohen, Now Found Publishing, LLC.

Published by Now Found Publishing, LLC Southlake, Texas

NowFoundPublishing.com

Trade Paperback ISBN: 978-1-942362-10-4

eBook ISBN: 978-1-942362-11-1

Original 2013 ISBN 978-0-9847138-5-1

First Printed in 2013

Published in the United States of America

1. Religion / General
2. Biography & Autobiography / Religious

16.10.20

Contents

Dedication

My forever love,

because of you

I understand hope, connection,

and the beauty of life.

You are the joy in my smile,

and the passion of my heart.

Because of you, I arise.

Dear Rosa,
You are blessed, beloved,
and treasured!
Michele Francesca

Foreword

It was a wonderful moment early one evening when I picked up the manuscript to *ARISE* by Michele Francesca Cohen. As a voracious reader who regularly digests several books per week, it is rare to be so fully captivated by one that keeps me up into the early morning hours. The reasons this book will bless you are threefold and all are centered in the marvelous grace of God manifested in the person of Michele Francesca Cohen.

The first is simply the revelation it contains. The great need in the church and the world today is for revelation. Jesus spoke of this revelation in His majestic response to Simon Peter's potent confession.

"Blessed are you, Simon Barjonah, because flesh and blood did not reveal this to you, but My Father who is in heaven. And I also say to you that you are Peter, and upon this rock I will build My church, and the gates of Hades will not overpower it."

Matthew 16:17–18, NASB —

We will never become the church Jesus promised to build without revelation. Principles and applications do not scare the enemy of the church, but revelation allows us to prevail over the very gates of hell. The book you hold in your hand is full of this kind of revelation. Michele shares with us the kind of revelation that only comes from heaven—revelation that will cause you to arise to your place of inheritance in the kingdom.

The second is the experience this message is built upon. When I was a seminary student a wise, older pastor told me, "A person should never write a book until they are at least forty years old or have had to bury someone they loved." I'm certain that advice is not canonical, but I have certainly appreciated the wisdom it contains. There are too many pointless books written by people who haven't weighed their words in the light of wilderness experiences, but *ARISE* is not one of them.

Michele Francesca Cohen is a woman who has been tested by fire; the genuineness of her faith is evident. You will find in these chapters golden truths that have been refined by the fire.

The third is the passion out of which it is written. Michele writes from a vulnerable and transparent life that exudes the passion of a real and authentic relationship with God. I have prayed with Michele and a person cannot hide their passion when they pray. I have listened to Michele minister the Scriptures and I know, each and every time, my heart will be stirred by her intensity in rightly dividing the Word of Truth. This book is born of a passionate life rich with experiences of the living God.

As you get ready to sit down and open these pages, I hope your appetite is sufficiently set on the edge of expectancy. Prepare to feast as Michele Francesca Cohen calls us to leave behind our medicinal messiahs and substitute saviors, and *arise* to our maximum potential for the glory of God.

Barry Clingan—
Senior Pastor, The Church at Trophy Lakes
Trophy Club, Texas

Introduction

We all have a story to tell. Each individual tale is unique and fascinating, and mine is no exception. Valiant ventures in twenty-one countries spanning over three decades in the worlds of sport, art, marriage, ministry, motherhood, and more have all added up to a story not unlike yours—one that is brimming over with trials, triumphs, brokenness, bravery, hopes deferred, and desires fulfilled. Within the pages of this book, you will find a story you can relate to, written by someone as down-to-earth and as real as you are—someone who knows what it is to walk through difficult times yet arise out of them in resurrection strength.

I've chosen to share my story with transparency because I believe people are looking for something real. They're looking for real because they want to *be* real. They want the freedom to acknowledge when they're hurting and not be judged for it—to be given room to relate to God, themselves, and others in an intimate and authentic way. Not only do people want to be real in their brokenness, they want to be armed with wisdom and power. They want useful tools they can harness in challenging circumstances—tools that can help them become a better, stronger version of themselves both in spite of their trials and because of them.

Above all, people are hungry to experience true and lasting transformation from the inside out. They want to know who they are, where they come from, and what they're here for. Right now, people all over the planet are longing to be validated in their value, inaugurated in their identity, and positioned in their purpose. If that's your desire, you've come to the right place. *ARISE* contains the keys and steps that can equip you to soar to new heights of personal freedom and fulfillment. It's a spiritual road map—a journey of intention to take you from faith to faith, strength to strength, and glory to glory. Along the way, you'll find rest stops—opportunities to dig deep, process, transition, and grow. For some, the pilgrimage will be fast-paced. For others, a slower tempo will be needed to give time for contemplation and application.

As we walk out our diverse pathways of transformation, it's likely we all have at least one thing in common: an aspiration to arise. The word *arise* means "to get up" and "to ascend," (the movement toward a source or a beginning). Arise also means "to come into being"— to experience the wonder of our true selves in glorious, authentic freedom. Now is your appointed time to do just that—to arise from your wounds, shake off your ashes, know your value, walk in your freedom, live in your vitality, put on your strength, and lift up your voice. Now is your time to *ARISE.*

1
Arise From Your Wounds

Potential

One thing we can be sure of in this beautiful world is difficult times will come and go. Sloughs of despond, furnaces of affliction—call them what we will—trials and tribulations can hurt us deeply. Some tough times are so overwhelming they can leave us feeling robbed of motivation and incapable of taking another step forward. They can leave us feeling so low, it's a struggle to even get up.

Most of us know what it's like to walk through painful trials of one kind or another. Rejection, abuse, loss, neglect, violation, betrayal… Experiences such as these can be devastating to our hearts and leave us wondering if we'll ever be the same again. The chances are we won't be—all our experiences transform us to some degree. But it's important to be aware that when painful wounds are left untended, they have the potential to cause "infection" in our souls—infection that can go deep, causing long-term struggles and serious side effects. If treated with wisdom, however, our agonizing wounds can achieve for us "an eternal weight of glory far beyond all comparison" (2 Corinthians 4:17, NASB). They have the potential to become our sunrise after a long, dark night, our window to a new perspective, and the springboard by which we can arise in genuine strength.

Loss

Of all the wounds we suffer in a lifetime, loss is one of the most difficult to navigate. It carves, in its cruel wake, a sizable vacuum within our tender, stricken souls. Loss is both formidable and intimidating in all its various forms. The fact that we can recall our losses and rejections with any degree of clarity (regardless of how much time has passed) is proof of the hefty toll they can take on our hearts. One insignificant, yet vivid, memory of loss from my childhood still remains with me to this day.

The incident took place on a Saturday while I was out with my parents at our hometown mall in England. Christmas had only just passed, but the streets were packed with eager shoppers hunting for end-of-season bargains. Typically, our family shopping trips could be a bit of a drag, but on this crisp winter morning, I had a wonderful new diversion to keep me entertained: a pair of the most diva-deluxe, faux fur mittens any young celebrity wannabe could hope for! My parents had a knack for buying fabulous girlie gifts that made me feel like a pretty, young princess or a glamorous movie star. This most exciting accoutrement was certainly no exception. The luxurious, soft brown fur captured my attention and stirred my six-year-old imaginations in a myriad of fairytale ways. Aware that the mittens had not yet been attached to my coat sleeves, my watchful mother cautioned me to be protective of my treasured new accessory; she knew I'd be heartbroken if they got lost.

Later that morning in Woolworths department store, as we meandered slowly toward the cheese counter, I noticed a clearance bin filled with half-priced books. The cover of a colorful, illustrated pop-up caught my eye; I felt it warranted immediate investigation. Realizing that small motor dexterity would be necessary to turn the pages, I removed my mittens and carefully placed them on the pile of books in front of me. Within moments, I was carried away to enchanted castles and magical kingdoms in imaginary, faraway lands. All too abruptly, the familiar voice of my father brought me back down to earth. "Come on, darling," he called. "Time to go." We were moving on. Dawdling meant running the risk of being left behind. Hurriedly, I put the book back in the bin and stuffed the mittens into my coat pocket. I was eager to feel the security of my daddy's hand as we navigated our way through the thick crowd of shoppers that towered around me.

When all the errands were run, we headed back to the car. Before long, we were winding our way through the tree-lined avenues that led to home. It was then that I remembered my mittens. In one determined movement, I stuffed my hands into my coat pockets to retrieve the beautiful treasures and adore them all over again. My right hand was immediately comforted by soft, silky fur, but my left hand grasped at empty space, cookie crumbs, and an old plastic candy wrapper. I grappled around, distraught and frightened. Tears were already stinging my eyes as my mind attempted to grasp the impossible: I had lost one of my mittens! I can still remember the pain I experienced in losing something valuable and precious, yes, even a faux fur mitten. My little heart was torn.

Good Grief

There is *some* truth to the cliché "time heals all things," but whether it's a loved one, a relationship, a hope, or a dream, if that which is now irreplaceable was once an intricate part of our affections, time can seem irrelevant and heal little. It is wise, therefore, not to belittle the reality of pain that occurs from traumas, trials, and tribulations. Most of us are faced with several losses in our lifetime. Some tear our hearts more severely than others leaving deep wounds and emotional scar tissue, even for years to come.

Sometimes we're too hasty to stuff away the pain that results from distressing events. Abandoned pain that finds no outlet for grief can become like a cluttered pile of damaged and tangled emotions within our hearts—a stagnant pool of sorrow that hinders us from feeling and responding healthfully in our relationships.

If we want to heal well, it's important we recognize that there is such a thing as *good grief*—grief that allows us to touch, acknowledge, and mourn our losses, and to process our pain with understanding.

Please know, I'm not advocating prolonged seasons of morbid introspection—life really does go on. But considering the anguish I felt over the loss of a mitten, it's little wonder we struggle with indescribable heartache over the deeper matters of our lives. Too often, the modern-day tyranny of the urgent requires that we soldier on in our brokenness with a plastic smile, all the while resorting to cleverly crafted coping methods to mask our unhealed pain and ailing, internal conditions. Midst the busyness and demands of life, some wounds and struggles can become deeply buried beneath the surface of our day-to-day existence. Though out of sight, these disquieting memories are like a nagging discomfort in the fabric of our souls, eating up our vitality and leaving us devoid of genuine joy.

An Incurable Wound

After reading the book of Jeremiah, specifically chapter 30, I found myself wondering if there is such a thing as an incurable wound—a brokenness deep within caused by an affliction, a hurtful experience, a hope deferred, or a shattered dream. I could certainly relate to the idea that there is. I, myself, once incurred a wound that felt so devastating, it seemed as though it was without remedy or cure.

God *is* love; we can be certain of that. The sovereign Creator has never been the source of our suffering and never will be. Yet it seems that seasons of difficulty are permitted for us to endure, often without speedy conclusions. Perhaps then, it is not unreasonable to suggest that some sufferings come our way for a specific, redemptive purpose.

In Jeremiah chapter 30, God speaks to the nation of Israel saying,

> *Your wound is incurable, and your injury is serious. There is no one to plead your cause; no healing for your sore, no recovery for you. All your lovers have forgotten you, they do not seek you; For I have wounded you with the wound of an enemy, with the punishment of a cruel one… Why do you cry out over your injury… I have done these things to you.*

Jeremiah 30:12–15, NASB —

A Better Plan

This passage does not seem to indicate that Israel's iniquities (and subsequent punishment) led to her abandonment. Only a few lines earlier, Jeremiah 30:11 (NASB) says, "'For I am with you,' declares the Lord, 'to save you.'" Perhaps then, the punishment spoken of in these verses was a prevention-is-better-than-cure strategy to deter the nation from its wayward tendencies.

We all need deterrents at times, not necessarily because we're wayward, but because, subconsciously or otherwise, we're set on a course of action that could lead us astray from God's *better* plan— the plan he sees but we don't. In such cases, God might allow us to undergo challenging trials by which he can bring about a better outcome for our lives.

Within the caverns of our hearts, many of us bear the agonies of incurable wounds that we rarely speak of—betrayals, rejections, abuses, cruel separations, disappointments, disablements—wounds that bleed internally, maybe even for decades, often without our comprehension as to their deeper, redemptive purpose.

We need to remember that God doesn't do bad things to us, yet at times, the all-wise Spirit allows a bitter, cold wind to blow through our lives. Though it might hurt us deeply, a capacity resides within us to withstand and to learn from our sufferings. Simply put, God allows challenging times in our lives to pave the way for us to become a better version of ourselves, both in spite of our trials and because of them. While they're happening, difficult trials make little sense within the finite realms of our limited understanding. Sadly, as a result, many of us spend too much time resenting the troublesome events of our lives, questioning God's sovereignty, doubting his love, and looking back in regret on what should have been but wasn't.

Somehow, we need to see our hurting condition as an *opportunity* to abort our anesthetizing cover-up tactics—those well-meaning good works we employ to glamorize our external appearance while ignoring the deeper root causes of our internal dis-ease. We need to seize the chance to connect to our own hearts and engage in authentic relationship with the gracious Lover of our souls. Only he can take what was meant for our demise and turn it around for good.

One-Upmanship

Perhaps you're familiar with the story of Jacob in the book of Genesis. This ambitious grandson of Abraham experienced an incurable wound that worked a deep and transforming work in his heart. As the second-born twin, Jacob grew up knowing he'd missed out on the family birthright by seconds. He was also aware that his brother, Esau, was the favorite in the eyes of their dad. We can't be certain, but it's possible these second place, runner-up, childhood experiences fueled Jacob's desire for a callous game of one-upmanship with his older sibling. As he was raised, Jacob probably heard much about the blessings and promises of God. Clearly, his sights became fixed on obtaining them.

One day, after Esau returned home from a hunt, Jacob took cunning advantage of his brother's weary and famished condition. Recognizing that his brother was so starved that he thought he might die, Jacob persuaded Esau to sell him his birthright in exchange for a bowl of stew. Esau fell for the trap and ate the food. Once the strengthening nutrients hit Esau's bloodstream and he was able to reason more clearly, I imagine he was furious with himself and with Jacob for allowing such a thing to happen. Genesis 25:34 (NASB) tells us, "Esau despised his birthright."

As if that wasn't enough, Jacob's mother encouraged her youngest son to steal Esau's firstborn blessing as well. Jacob accomplished this by preparing his father's favorite food in the way Esau typically prepared it. He then put on a hairy garment so he would smell like Esau. When Jacob fed the meal to his blind, aging father, Isaac perceived Jacob to be the older son.

Unintentionally, Isaac gave his patriarchal blessing to Jacob saying,

> *May many nations become your servants, and may they bow down to you. May you be the master over your brothers, and may your mother's sons bow down to you. All who curse you will be cursed, and all who bless you will be blessed.*
>
> Genesis 27:29, NLT —

Once the blessing was given, it was irrevocable.

Something Missing

This trickery and feuding was the backdrop for a head-to-head confrontation between Jacob and Esau years later. Soon after he received his father's blessing, Jacob left the family home in fear of his brother's fury and vengeance. Many years later, Esau came to seek out his brother accompanied by four hundred men. When Jacob heard of this, he was "greatly afraid and distressed" (Genesis 32:7, NASB). Jacob sent servants to offer gifts to Esau and his men saying, "I will appease him with the present that goes before me. Then afterward I will see his face; perhaps he will accept me" (Genesis 32:20, NASB).

Jacob had lawfully obtained both the birthright and his father's irrevocable blessing, yet it is evident from these Scriptures that Jacob wasn't behaving in the self-assured way one might expect from a man with so much spiritual treasure in his possession. Jacob's plan was to appease Esau in hopes of experiencing a sense of acceptance—

something he probably felt was lacking in his life since early childhood, perhaps most especially from his father. But appeasement is just another way of medicating the *symptoms* of a problem as opposed to dealing with the problem at its root. *Accept* in Hebrew is *nacah*, which means "to arise." Jacob was seeking for a sense of acceptance by which to *come into being*. Instead of embracing the unconditional approval and acceptance of God, Jacob sought acceptance from another source—in this case, his brother.

Survival Tactics

Appeasement and people pleasing to gain approval and acceptance are behaviors that indicate deep-rooted insecurity. When someone is insecure and unsure of their identity and personhood, it's a telltale sign they feel like something's missing—that there's a fundamental lack within them—that they're not good enough or not *enough*. Insecurity is "code" for "I'm not lovable." No doubt this was a core belief that formed deep down in Jacob's subconscious as he grew up playing second fiddle to his big brother, Esau.

Jacob's go-to survival tactic was manipulation. Instead of securely relying on God's provision and goodness, he sought to secure his future by manipulating people and situations. Scripture shows that God had always intended for Jacob to be a patriarch of Israel. No doubt Jacob had an intuitive sense of his God-ordained destiny from childhood, yet instead of allowing his dynamic calling to be brought about in God's way and time, Jacob yielded to fear and took matters into his own hands.

Manipulating circumstances to feel good about ourselves and to get what we want only ever provides temporary solutions for our inner fears. Jacob discovered this to be true on the eve of his confrontation with Esau. His internal world was on shaky ground. Though he had "everything," it was as though he had nothing. (Only that which is given to us by God is truly ours to steward and enjoy.) Everything about Jacob's insecure response to Esau's arrival suggests that it's possible to have a head knowledge of our birthright and blessings, yet not have true ownership of them in our hearts.

Jacob, certain his brother meant him harm, hurriedly ushered the women and children out of danger's way by taking them across the Jabbok River at nightfall. Jacob, however, remained to face his brother. Genesis 32:24 (NASB) says, "Then Jacob was left alone." In Hebrew, the word *left* means "jut over, exceed, or too much." It indicates Jacob was at a point in his life where he had reached the end of his rope—"jutting out" on the edge of his own frailty—lonely, desperate, and afraid. I can almost hear him whisper in the darkness, "This one's too much for me, God. It's more than I can handle!" No doubt, many of us can relate to the confusion Jacob felt that night. I remember hitting rock bottom in a similar way years ago through an incident that caught me completely off guard. It was the last thing in the world I ever expected to happen.

One More Time

About a year after graduating from the Doreen Bird College of Performing Arts, in Kent, England, I met an amazing man and fell head over heels in love. For me, it was love at first sight. I was smitten to the core from the earliest moments of our connection. We saw each other as often as we could and it wasn't long before we were talking about the possibility of marriage. We often wiled away the night hours "planning" our exotic honeymoon on a romantic island beach. We shared many beautiful, intimate moments together. Unaccustomed as I was to the concept of saving myself for my husband-to-be, it would be honest to say, I gave this man my all. In my heart, I was committed to him completely. I felt certain there was no one else for me but him and I believed we would be together forever. I loved him deeply and passionately, and he loved me too. But in our second year of dating, I can only imagine his heart must have grown cold toward me. Whatever was going on, he hid it well. If there were any warning signs of what was about to happen, I'd failed to notice them. Little did I know, I was about to be blindsided by one of the most wrenching experiences of my entire life.

One Sunday afternoon, as we drove back to my digs after a lovely day out, my boyfriend suddenly shut down on me. He refused to speak to me or even look in my direction. I had no idea what had brought on such arctic behavior. I was bewildered and scared. By the time we reached my street, I was pleading for him to communicate. By the time we reached the driveway, I heard myself saying, "If you don't look at me or speak to me before I get out of this car, I'll have to assume you're breaking up with me."

To my utter horror, despite all the beautiful and intimate times we'd shared together, he continued to look straight ahead refusing to respond. I was forced to get out of the car, close the door, and watch him drive away without so much as offering me a backward glance. That day, without any explanation whatsoever, I watched the man to whom I'd given my body, heart, and soul disappear out of my life.

Bleeding Heart

To say I was heartbroken is an understatement. I was completely crushed and remained so for years to come. My heartache seemed incurable; the pain I felt was agonizing. I learned to carry on but failed to appropriately grieve my loss and redefine life without the man I loved. My soul continued to hemorrhage. The deep wound refused to heal.

My haphazard attempts at recovery (which included a series of short-lived, meaningless, rebound relationships) neither masked the tormenting pain nor allowed sufficient time for the wound to mend. Scar tissue became the mainstay of my heart's substance. Worst of all, I didn't re-establish the truth that I was indeed a beautiful woman worthy of far greater respect than had been shown to me through my boyfriend's thoughtless actions. My failure at that time to learn crucial lessons concerning my value and identity led to much unnecessary suffering in the decades that followed. Instead of processing my pain and allowing it to work for good, I attempted to anesthetize my discomfort every way I knew how. One thing became clear to me in the years after that breakup: no drug, food, gig, job, religion, party, or one-night stand can heal the agony of a broken heart or fill the void of an empty one. It's sad to say, but in my search for relief, I tried just about all of them. What I needed most was a divine intervention.

There Must Be More

Back at the Jabbok River, God was fully aware of Jacob's anguish and despair. Having delivered his family to safety, Jacob was left alone to face both himself and the anticipated fury of his soon-to-arrive brother. But it wasn't long before an unexpected guest showed up on Jacob's doorstep: The Angel of the Lord. Some Bible versions describe the Angel of the Lord as a man, yet most scholars agree, the Angel of the Lord referred to in this passage of scripture was actually the Lord himself. What's interesting here is that this heaven-sent visitor did not come to console Jacob in his anguish; he came to wrestle with him. It was a lengthy confrontation that lasted until daybreak. Jacob was accustomed to fighting for his survival and this night was no exception.

The book of Genesis says of the Angel:

When he saw that he had not prevailed against him, he

touched the socket of his thigh; so the socket of his thigh
was dislocated while he wrestled with him. Then he said,
"Let me go, for the dawn is breaking." But he said, "I will
not let you go unless you bless me."

Genesis 32:25–26, NASB —

Much is revealed through Jacob's heart-cry, "I will not let you go unless you bless me." Though he appeared to be blessed with everything he needed, Jacob knew there must be more! The blessings he had obtained up until that point were predominantly through his own strength and manipulation. Jacob knew he needed a blessing that came directly from God's own heart to his—a blessing that would touch him at a far deeper level than anything he'd ever experienced before. He needed a blessing that could transform him from the inside out and give him an unshakable security and identity that no man or circumstance could take from him. What was true for Jacob is also true for us: In order to face our past with grace and our future with assurance, we need genuine heart revelation about who we are, not just head knowledge about what we have.

Inside Out

It was audacious of Jacob to cling to God until he blessed him, but that didn't shake the Rock of Ages. Audacity and tenacity are what it will take to shift us from a stuck, mediocre existence into the abundant life God intends for us. God is waiting on *us* to come to him with the same kind of determination Jacob had. If we don't have an absolute assurance of our identity and security in God, we need to wrestle for it until we do!

Sadly today, there seems to be a myriad of people who have a legal kingdom birthright, yet they don't live like they're God's child. They understand with their minds that they're blessed, but fear, distrust, and unbelief still play a dominant role in their hearts. God knows we're in danger of latching onto an *idea* of who he is while relating to him from a religious distance. Doing this prevents us from coming into a genuine sense of security from the inside out. Just as in Jacob's life, our heavenly Father allows us to come to the end of our own strength, even if it causes us pain in the process. He allows it so that we'll cry out to him for his inimitable touch, and experience lasting, life-changing transformation.

Transition by Transformation

God met Jacob at his point of desperation that night and blessed him with unshakable blessings. Those blessings, however, came at a price. As they wrestled, God inflicted Jacob with a wound. Genesis 32:25 (NASB) describes how the Angel of the Lord "touched the socket of his thigh." *Touched* in Hebrew is *naga*, which means "reached, punished," or "brought down." *Socket* is *kaph*, which means "middle, power," or "place of strength." (*Kaph*, incidentally, is from the root word *kaphaph*, which means "to bow down"). In Hebraic language, the thigh represents the place in the body involved in reproduction. Paraphrased in a way we can better understand, Genesis 32:25 tells us that the place of Jacob's own power and strength—the place from which he would reproduce himself—was reached, touched, and brought down by the hand of God.

Jacob hadn't yet crossed over the Jabbok to head toward Canaan, but I believe God was pleased to hold his beloved son back from the Promised Land a little while longer. The meaning of *Jabbok* in the original Hebrew language is "to empty itself" and "the place of passing over." God didn't want Jacob to enter into the Promised Land in the unstable spiritual condition he was in, relying on his own strength and manipulative ways, and living out of usurped blessings that were hand-me-down head knowledge. He wanted Jacob to be emptied of his old mindsets so that he could pass over into the promises of God, transformed from the inside out. He wanted Jacob to have an inherent experience of identity and sonship and an unshakable ownership of God's blessings in his heart. In the same way that Jacob was held back from "passing over" into the Promised Land, God will sometimes hold us back from the next level of our destiny if we're stuck in old patterns of behavior. This is especially the case if those patterns are hurtful to us or to others. Sooner or later, we must to be transformed from the inside out if we hope to arise in our fullest potential. What applied to Jacob applies to us: there's no true transition without genuine transformation.

Divine Dislocation

We can attempt to dodge and hide from our painful dilemmas or seek temporary escape from the reality of our relational mess-ups, but dragging around our insecure selves and unresolved issues everywhere we go is an unnecessary burden we need not bear. Our journey would be so much lighter and brighter if our excess internal baggage of fears, dysfunctions, addictions, self-reliance, and codependent tendencies were unpacked and left behind forever. It may take a wrestling match with God and some focused help, but the outcome will be well worth the temporary discomfort involved.

God, in his mercy and wisdom, reached, touched, and brought down Jacob's own iniquitous power and strength *before* allowing him to go into the Promised Land. God knew he must dislocate something deep within Jacob so he could reset it the right way. God did this so that Jacob could experience the full benefit of the blessings he'd been given. The Ancient of Days didn't delight in Jacob's pain, but he knew it would take an incurable wound to bring him into a place of genuine spiritual connection and identity (both for Jacob's own sake and for the sake of his descendants).

Change for the Better

From the time his hip became dislocated, Jacob was unable to operate with ease in his own strength. He limped away from his wrestling experience never to walk the same way again. Yet it was this very injury that gave Jacob an unshakable assurance of God's blessings in his life—an assurance he would take with him from that day forward into every situation he faced. Jacob's incurable wound became a memorial to his own transformation—the defining moment that forever enriched his relationship with God, himself, and others. As he transitioned into the Promised Land emptied of his own strength, it's likely Jacob regarded this night of wounding as both the worst *and* the best experience of his life.

When we're in the midst of struggles, we tend to see them as a curse, but God knows they will ultimately work together for our good (Romans 8:28). In times of trial, we strive with God, pleading with him to make the cloudy days bright and to make us comfortable again. But God knows at the end of our dark and difficult night, the light of a new dawn will be shining, and we will understand what we couldn't understand before. We will see for ourselves: the trials that we feared would destroy us were the same trials that prepared us to steward God's blessings more responsibly. They were the opportunities that prepared us for our destiny and calling.

Our trials are our "wrestling match" moments. If we see them through to their full conclusion, we will arise changed for the better. Sadly, when my boyfriend left me in the cruel way he did, I didn't hear my wake-up call. I didn't recognize my heartache to be the internal limp that could have and should have caused me to walk a new and better way. Nevertheless, God was at work in my situation, faithfully leading me toward my own Jabbok experience.

Doorway of Hope

At the time of my break up, I was working as a professional choreographer and dancer in London's prestigious West End theater district. I was also a teacher and choreographer at The Italia Conti Academy of Theater Arts in London. My work was creative and exciting. Vocationally, I was doing what I loved. But despite a successful career and an external appearance of well-being and prosperity, my heart was in shreds.

Like Jacob on the night before Esau confronted him, I knew I'd arrived at the end of my rope. The devastating effect of my "incurable wound" and the self-destructive means by which I'd attempted to medicate my pain had driven me to the darkest corner of my existence. In short, I contemplated suicide. Hopeless and hurting, I broke down in racking sobs at the foot of my bed. Though I don't expect for one moment God delighted to see me so full of sorrow, it was this utter despair that delivered me to a doorway of hope that night. What happened next was completely unexpected.

Though my father is Catholic and my mother Protestant (with Jewish ancestors), my family didn't participate in any kind of religious services during my growing up years. My only brush with spirituality had been the weekly recitation of the Lord's Prayer in school assembly. Yet from the very depths of my brokenness, I heard myself cry aloud these wonderful words: "Jesus, if you're real, please help me!"

To this day, I still don't know what prompted me to call on the Savior's name; perhaps a distant and compassionate soul had noticed my sadness and was praying for me. I cried for hours that night until there were no tears left to cry. Empty and exhausted, I scraped myself off the floor and prepared for bed the way I usually did during that dark and depressing season: by rolling and smoking a joint—the only practice I knew of at the time that could calm my troubled mind.

Something Different

Morning arrived all too soon. Hung over from marijuana, I staggered around pulling myself together for work. Despite my cry for help the previous night, nothing seemed to have changed. One thing, however, was new. It was an idea that I couldn't seem to shake off—to work extra hours and save money to travel somewhere I'd never been before. Australia, Canada, and the west coast of America all came to mind as possible destinations. As the weeks passed, my musings of travel intensified and I felt compelled to venture toward the unknown.

I approached my boss to ask for a four-month sabbatical from my teaching position at the theater arts academy. To my amazement, not only did she grant me a leave of absence (while holding my position until the next semester), but she also connected me with her good friend, Francis Chapman in California, a former choreographer for the Jackson 5. Francis kindly offered to host me in her home during my stay in the United States. Everything seemed to be falling into place, so I booked a flight and prepared for my overseas adventure.

A few months later, with cash stowed in my carry-on and savings in my account at home, I boarded a plane for LAX. Francis met me at the airport and drove me to her house in Van Nuys. She had the most beautiful smile and gracious demeanor and immediately went out of her way to help me feel safe and cared for. Weeks later, I discovered Francis had suffered a terrible personal tragedy shortly before my arrival. But in her loving concern for me, she never once mentioned her own bereavement and pain. It was as though she was connected to a divine Source of strength and compassion—a Source I was about to encounter in a personal way for the very first time.

As the jet lag wore off, a quiet, internal panic set in. I was fairly well traveled from my sport and artistic days, but life in California was different to anything I'd experienced before. Culture shock hit me in a big way. There I was in a stranger's house, far away from everything that was familiar to me, not quite sure what to do next. Maybe my idea of just showing up in a foreign country without a job, plan, or purpose wasn't so smart after all. Little did I know, however, a plan had already been made for me.

Coming Home

Two days after my arrival, early on a Sunday morning, I stirred awake as Francis crept into the room where I was sleeping. She was getting ready to go out and needed something from the closet. "Where are you going?" I asked her quietly, eyes barely open. "To church," she replied gently, with a smile.

I heard myself sheepishly requesting to join her. I had no idea what I was in for. My only experience with church up until that time had been about a year earlier in London when I wandered into a stone, cold, historic church building during an unattended daytime hour. I had exited hastily; the embellished altars and stained-glass windows depicting figures from a bygone age all seemed meaningless to me. My first experience of church in America, however, was about to be entirely different.

Within the hour, Francis and I were walking down the center aisle of Church on the Way, pastored by the legendary Dr. Jack Hayford. My kind, new friend had arranged to meet her film actress comrade, Diane Venora, at the service, so she ventured off to find her, promising that she would return promptly and get us seated. As I waited, I became aware of a beautiful presence all around me. It was unlike anything I'd ever felt before. I was at the time, and still am, highly sensitive to environments both spiritual and physical. In my teenage years, I had dabbled in the occult. The contrast of spiritual atmospheres from those Ouija board encounters to the light-filled energy at Church on the Way was starkly evident to me. I was moved to tears and felt wrapped in peace. Instinctively I knew that I was standing in the holy presence of God.

As I stood there alone, surrounded by people singing joyful songs of praise, I heard a voice speak to my heart. I still remember it as being the most gentle and truthful voice I'd ever heard. "It's alright, Michele," he said. You're home now, you're home." I can't explain how, but I knew immediately it was the voice of Jesus. I continued to feel wrapped in loving warmth all day, and tears continued to stream down my cheeks. Something very powerful was happening to me.

A New Heart

After the service, we ate lunch out and then dropped Diane at The Beverly Hills Hotel on Sunset Boulevard. For the entire afternoon, I behaved like a social misfit, weeping quietly, barely able to eat or speak. Around five o'clock, Francis took me back to Church on the Way for a special evening service featuring international evangelists, John Jacobs and The Power Team. At hearing John's dynamic message, my heart was touched deeply and I began to grasp the meaning of the "Welcome Home" words I'd heard earlier that day. I understood for the first time that Jesus died so I wouldn't have to. I understood that he took the punishment for all my wrongs. I understood that he rose from the dead to give me eternal life. I learned that I could leave the past behind and receive a new life in Christ. That night, I gave my broken, tattered life to Jesus. In exchange, I received a new heart and a new beginning. I knew immediately, my eternity was settled and I was loved with an everlasting love.

I can honestly say, I became a new creation that night, and I've walked with my beloved Savior ever since. Did my heartache from the past disappear entirely that day? No, unfortunately not. Finding genuine freedom from such deep-rooted pain was to be a process that would take many more years yet to come. But at least now, I was in a place where I could be better equipped to embrace the lessons I needed to learn. My first love had left me on the side of the road, rejected and broken with a cruelly inflicted wound. But the wound that broke me ultimately led me to Jesus—the one who will never leave me or forsake me—the one who is my light and my salvation, my Redeemer and my Healer, the true and trustworthy Lover of my soul.

Walking with a Limp

It took something very painful to turn my life right-side up. Perhaps it has been the same for you. No matter who we are or what stage of life we're in, our wounds and challenges can bring us into a better place if we embrace them as a providential gift. Arising from wounds is not about wishing bad things away or numbing down our feelings to pretend that everything is fine. To arise from our wounds, we must recognize that the difficult situations we face *can* be used for our greater good.

The key to arising from wounds is our perspective toward the things that cause us pain. Have you ever heard the saying "no pain, no gain?" It isn't comfortable, but it's true. We have a choice either to see our wounds as insurmountable obstacles that are certain to bring about our demise, or to recognize them as gifts that can effectively prepare us for our future. We can allow our struggles to become an excuse for bitterness, or we can embrace them as stepping-stones to arising in strength.

Jacob's dislocated hip caused him to limp for the rest of his life.

Wherever he went, he leaned upon his staff. Similarly, our dislocated hearts will cause us to "limp" on the inside. This internal limp gives us an opportunity to lean more heavily on the strength of God and to draw from the certainty of a supernatural Source. When we have an internal limp, we live our lives at a slower pace. We take time to enjoy the blessings we've been given and the beauty that surrounds us. We're less able to run ahead of God. Instead, we walk by his side and experience the closeness of his presence. We rest our hand confidently in his as he steadies us over life's road bumps.

Without the gift of challenges and trials, we tend to race along life's highway at full speed, relying on our own strength and wisdom, obsessed with our own egos, cutting corners, and treading on anyone who gets in our way. Our internal or external limps confront us with our own imperfections and prompt us to tolerantly offer mercy to those in need of comfort. We come to realize that the distance we cover in our race is measured less by our own external accomplishments and more by the depth of our genuine love for God and our fellow man.

Kingdom Keys

My heart breaks for the countless souls who have suffered, and continue to suffer, inhumane pain and unspeakable loss. Some woes of heartache seem mild in comparison to the horror and tragedy suffered by others, yet levels of private pain cannot be objectively graphed or defined on a scale of intensity. Our internal sufferings and heartaches cannot be compared to the sufferings of another. Neither can we arise from our own despair on the basis that someone else has been through something worse. We're best inspired to arise from our wounds by looking to the Redeemer of our souls who knows firsthand what it is to go through hell and back.

The greatest arisings start from the lowest places. The Savior proved it:

> *What does "he ascended" mean except that he also*
> *descended to the lower, earthly regions? He who*
> *descended is the very one who ascended higher than all*
> *the heavens, in order to fill the whole universe.*
>
> Ephesians 4:9–10, NIV —

On his descent into hell, Jesus took hold of the Keys of the Kingdom. When we hit rock bottom in our lives, it's also for a reason. If we're going to go "through hell and back" we should make the journey worthwhile by taking hold of kingdom keys, just as Jesus did, even in our lowest moments. These are the keys of victory and authority over darkness in Jesus's name—the keys of wisdom and understanding that are forged in our hearts during challenging seasons. It is these keys that empower us to arise from our wounds.

Kingdom keys are given into our hands to unlock the potential within our own hearts. They are also given to us for the "opening of the prison to those who are bound" (Isaiah 61:1 ESV). As we endure through our own losses and versions of "hell and back," we gain compassion, wisdom, and understanding by which we can help set others free. God "comforts us in all our troubles, so that we can comfort those in any trouble with the comfort we ourselves receive from God" (2 Corinthians 1:4, NIV).

Empowered to Arise

There are two ways to arise from our wounds. The first is in our own strength. Many of us have tried this approach to arising countless times only to discover our own strength fails us over and over again. When we buckle and fall, each collapse seems more overwhelming than the one before. Strength is essential, but superficial bravado can be our enemy, especially if we hide behind it to avoid dealing with the root causes of our pain or dysfunction. False strength keeps us in an emotional stalemate and prevents us from genuinely arising from our wounds.

The second and only way to *truly* arise from our wounds is through active, authentic connection with our own hearts and with the power and love of God. This is something we can experience when we face our wounds with courage, grieve our pain with honesty, and allow the lessons we've learned through our agonizing trials to be effectively applied to our hearts and lives.

Even though we may have experienced grave brokenness, we *can* experience Christ's resurrection power. No matter how long or how difficult our journeys may have been—no matter how many tears we've shed or how much pain we've endured— the same power that raised Jesus from the dead is able to raise us up too. The same arms that carried Jesus from hell to heaven will carry us also, and they won't let us go.

Come into Being

God wants us to arise, but in *genuine* wholeness. With open arms and a concerned heart, the Savior implores us to pour out our anguish, grieve our losses, and process our pain with honesty and authenticity. He encourages us to lay aside our survival tactics and cover-up bravado so that we can arise unhindered in resurrection strength. As we invite the Savior into the secret places of our hearts, he will give us courage to accept our limps. He will repair what is fractured and reset what is dislocated. He will give us grace to walk a new way. He will open the eyes of our hearts and help us to understand our trials from a heavenly perspective. He will build within us steadfast security that can only be found in his unconditional love.

As we embrace our pain as a necessary part of our destiny journey, the door to healing will be unlocked. As we recognize our unpleasant experiences as contrasts guiding us to make better choices, clarity is born. The energy we once expended to mask our insecurities will be redirected toward the establishing of our unshakable birthright. As we surrender to the process of authentic transformation, we will discover within ourselves an ability to appreciate our past and take responsibility for our future. We'll realize that had we not experienced our incurable wounds, we wouldn't be the people of substance, wisdom, and confidence that we are today.

Arising from wounds is more than just getting up and moving forward to leave the past behind. Arise means "to come into being"—to become all that we're destined and designed to be.

It is time to arise.

It is time to arise from your wounds.

Reflections

_____

_____

_____

_____

_____

_____

_____

_____

_____

_____

_____

_____

_____

_____

2
Shake Off Your Ashes

Memories

As a young girl, I had the distinct privilege of growing up in a quaint, suburban village in the beautiful county of Surrey, England. The sights and sounds and smells of those early years remain with me to this day as treasured recollections. I still remember with fondness the lush green countryside and towering oaks, the grand historic castles and country lanes, rose gardens, cobbled streets, noisy pubs, enchanting cafés... My list of wistful memories goes on and on.

Weekends were always my favorite. After a breakfast of soft-boiled eggs and soldiers, I would cheerfully wile away the hours riding my bike up and down the residential sidewalks. On many Sundays, we drove to Kent to visit my mother's parents. I loved listening to my grandad's chuckles and jovial jokes as the intoxicating smell of a sizzling roast wafted through his and Nanny's Bexleyheath duplex.

Summertime was a never-ending adventure. I can still hear the wake-up call of cooing pigeons and the late afternoon jingle of the ice cream van. Playing "house" in the woods was a warm weather staple. Bluebells in abundance carpeted my palaces in elegant style, and wild berries mixed with watery mud made a satisfying "vegetable soup." I also loved to play "theater" under my neighbor's weeping willow tree. The long, slender boughs were my imaginary stage curtains; I loved to fling open the branches and make dramatic entrances to center stage, wowing the "upper circle" with my captivating performances.

Christmases were always stupendous. It wasn't just the exchange of thoughtful gifts that made the holidays so special. It was the cake selections, the candied fruit, and the huge arrays of chocolates. Board games, Advent calendars, sparkly decorations, and Christmas crackers all played their part too.

Winters are long and hard in England, but the frosty bite of that bone-chilling season could in no way penetrate the coziness of our suburban semi-detached. Some of my fondest recollections as a child are of my mum and dad dancing in the living room to Frank Sinatra singing Cole Porter classics. Erroll Garner, Miles Davis, and more jazz greats than I've room here to mention were all part of my varied musical upbringing. My dad made sure all the classical composers were tucked in there too, not to mention all manners of pop and rock artists of the day. On Saturday nights, my brother and I loved to air-jam our hearts out donning eyeliner and dressing gowns while listening to the Top 40 on Radio One.

I'm grateful to say, my childhood years were filled with all kinds of heart-warming delights that still make me smile when I think of them today—family nights around the telly, rhubarb and custard sweets from the local newsagent, Enid Blyton paperback collections, fairytale bedtime stories, and all the beautiful growing up memories any little girl would be blessed to have experienced.

Bonfire Night

Another memory that still gives me the warm fuzzies to this day was the celebration of Guy Fawkes Day. In the United Kingdom, this historic event is commemorated each November 5th. Bonfire Night, or Fireworks Night as it's also known, is observed in England each year to commemorate the night in 1605 when Guy Fawkes was arrested. His crime: guarding explosives placed beneath the House of Lords for the purpose of assassinating King James I. To celebrate the bungle of the Gunpowder Plot and the king's survival from the murderous attempt on his life, people lit bonfires all around London. A few months later, the observance of an annual public day of thanksgiving was enforced as a reminder of the plot's failure.

As a young child, I was aware of the historic reasons for the Guy Fawkes celebration, but my favorite memories by far are of my family's backyard fireworks displays and my mum's delicious hot, buttery, sausage sandwiches served dripping with tomato ketchup. Typically, on the Saturday night closest to November 5th, local bonfires are lit in parks and fields. Entire communities turn out dressed in warm winter attire to watch their man-made "Guy" burn to a crisp atop a massive blaze of unwanted tree debris and fallen leaves. I'm sure this serves as a reminder to all Her Majesty's subjects even into the twenty-first century that treason is not a wise course of action!

The fifteen-foot high blazing outdoor furnaces were certainly a magnificent sight to behold, yet there was one feature of the extravaganzas I did *not* enjoy; the fact that I went home smelling of smoke. Ash would find its way into my clothes and my hair; the acrid smell even clung to my skin. It was a relief to get all cleaned up in the bath and put on fresh pajamas for bed.

Some Like It Hot

These memories of fire and heat remind me of a story in the book of Daniel that's especially appropriate for the subject of shaking off ashes. Chapter three recounts how three Hebrew exiles, Shadrach, Meshach, and Abednego, were tied up and thrown into a fiery furnace as punishment for not bowing down to Persian idols. The amazing outcome of the story is that they were delivered out of the fire without smelling of smoke and without displaying any evidence of the ordeal they'd just been through.

Before being thrown into the furnace, the courageous boys made it known that their devotion to God would not waver even if they were slain in their trial. Yet at the same time, they confidently proclaimed their belief that God could save them and bring them out of their furnace of affliction unscathed. King Nebuchadnezzar was so enraged by the audacity of their fearless stand that he heated the furnace seven times hotter than usual and had the three young men thrown into it.

He was really determined see them fry! But when the king looked into the fire, he was astounded to see a fourth man walking around with them, and they all appeared to be peaceful, protected, and safe.

He said, "Look! I see four men walking around in the fire, unbound and unharmed, and the fourth looks like a son of the gods." Nebuchadnezzar then approached the opening of the blazing furnace and shouted, "Shadrach, Meshach, and Abednego, servants of the Most High God, come out! Come here!" So, Shadrach, Meshach, and Abednego came out of the fire, and the satraps, prefects, governors, and royal advisers crowded around them. They saw that the fire had not harmed their bodies, nor was a hair of their heads singed; their robes were not scorched, and there was no smell of fire on them.

Then Nebuchadnezzar said, "Praise be to the God of Shadrach, Meshach, and Abednego, who has sent his angel and rescued his servants! They trusted in him and defied the king's command and were willing to give up their lives rather than serve or worship any god except their own God. Therefore I decree that the people of any nation or language who say anything against the God of Shadrach, Meshach and Abednego be cut into pieces and their houses be turned into piles of rubble, for no other god can save in this way." Then the king promoted Shadrach, Meshach and Abednego in the province of Babylon.

Daniel 3:25-30, NIV —

Refining Fire

Many of us have been through a furnace of affliction. We know what it is to see the flames of our fiery trials dance tormentingly before our eyes. A furnace of affliction feels like exactly that—an overwhelming furnace of emotional, psychological, or physical difficulty. It's a trial so harsh or lengthy it has the potential to burn us to the core and leave us in a metaphorical pile of smoldering ashes. But alternatively, as demonstrated by the three faithful Hebrew boys, our trials can be the fire through which our hearts and lives are refined to become like pure, transparent gold. Our faithfulness, fortitude, and humility during our ordeals can become acts of sacrificial worship both in the furnace and out. In the same way the faith of the Hebrew boys was tested, our faith will be tested also; our faith will be put on trial to reveal if it's genuine. It's an unavoidable process for any sincere follower of the Savior.

Our hearts become like genuine gold when we willingly embrace every aspect of our journey so that we might learn from our trials and shine transparently as a result. After the exiles were called out of the fire, King Nebuchadnezzar honored them for trusting in God. Then, he promoted them. If Shadrach, Meshach, and Abednego could come out of their fiery trials better off than when they went in, so can we!

Tribulations have the ability to incinerate our dreams, but our triumphant Savior is a master at taking our ashes and creating something new from them—something even better. He's able to reignite the desires of our heart and cause them to burn more brightly than we ever thought possible. As we discovered from the story of Jacob, God wants us to use our suffering as a doorway of connection to his provision, guidance, and favor. He wants us to enter our promised land with the full assurance of his blessings and promises.

God is with us in the testing flames just as he was with Shadrach, Meshach, and Abednego, but we have to look to him and find courage and reassurance from his nearness. We have to know that our God has not abandoned us, but "he will act like a refiner and a purifier of silver" (Malachi 3:3, GWT).

Skin Graft for the Soul

Furnaces of affliction can be opportunities—seasons of intense heat during which we allow the burning away of unhealthy habits, destructive behavior patterns, and unrefined characteristics—the things that hinder us from reaching our destiny. God has "new wine" to pour into us—purposeful vitality and enlightening perspectives that will empower us to live healthy and fulfilled lives. But new wine, Jesus instructed, must be contained in new containers:

No one puts new wine into old wine skins. For the old skins would burst from the pressure, spilling the wine and ruining the skins. New wine is stored in new wine skins so that both are preserved.

Matthew 9:17, NLT —

Old wine skins tear when they're filled with new wine. The costly contents spill and are wasted. Similarly, the precious wisdom gained through painful trials can be lost and wasted if we don't allow ourselves to be rebuilt into new "wine skins." The skin of burn victims is sometimes marred so severely that a skin graft is necessary to repair the damage. In the same way, our furnaces of affliction can be so intense that we become disfigured emotionally, psychologically, or spiritually. Trials of this degree can leave us needing a (wine skin) graft for our souls.

Though painful to endure, our willingness to allow a restoration "surgery" in our hearts and minds can yield remarkable results. By availing ourselves to a deep healing process, we can increase our capacity to assimilate wisdom gained in the heat of our battles, and thereby, be transformed. Our damaged souls can become reconstructed, and our hurting hearts can become healthy again, shining with the luster of resurrected identity.

Smelling of Smoke

To arise in our potential and come into being, we must allow our fiery trials to refine us, not consume us. Then, we must shake off our ashes and allow the pure, refined gold of our genuine faith to shine through us unhindered, "expressing itself through love" (Galatians 5:6, NIV).

As we walk through a recovery process, lingering memories and accumulated hurts from painful trials can be likened to ashes—the negative by-products of the positive good that was accomplished in us through the fire. The conscious or subconscious beliefs cultivated in our souls as a result of those trials are like burn scars. We "smell of smoke" when we reenact yesterday's trials over and over again in our thoughts, lifestyles, communication, and relationships. Whether hidden or obvious, ongoing patterns of anger, defensiveness, fear, withdrawal, or negativity are strong indications that we "smell of smoke" and that we're toting around some sensitive burn scars and ashes from the past that need to be shaken off.

To determine if we're carrying around ashes from the past, we must ask ourselves a few probing questions such as: Are the negative memories of my trials and experiences consuming my thoughts and affecting my decisions? Are my beliefs, thoughts, words, and actions governed or influenced by fear, anger, or distrust? Am I easily triggered into negative behavior patterns when things in my life appear to be going wrong? Have I become paralyzed by my past experiences, unable to embrace hope and vision for my future?

These are tough questions and may take considerable time to answer in depth, but in the same way a construction foreman needs to assess the damage incurred to a building after a fire, we also need to accurately assess the condition of our souls after a season of challenge or difficulty. The great news is, no matter how bad our experiences may have been, we *can* be rebuilt. Just as with Shadrach, Meshach, and Abednego, it's possible for us to come out of our furnaces of affliction without even the faintest smell of smoke lingering upon us.

Authentic Dreams

The flames of anguish, suffering, and trauma have a way of sucking the life out of us. It's as though the spiritual oxygen that once sourced our hope gets swallowed up in the heat of our overwhelming circumstances. When the fire cools down and only smoke and ash remain, we find ourselves gasping for the breath of life, longing for a sense of significance and yearning to dream dreams again. At vulnerable times such as these, we need to be careful not to rush our healing process by conjuring up false hopes devised out of unstable motives.

Virtual life "opportunities" bombard us through social media. IM and e-mail make easy pathways for engagement in fantasy worlds and Internet romances offering escape from the pressures and pains of life. These "relationships" can feel deceivingly genuine, yet bear little reference to everyday reality. Succumbing to the bait of these online temptations is like pitching a tent beside an active volcano; sooner or later, someone's going to get burned.

Whether in cyberspace or day-to-day life, eluding reality by living in an imaginary headspace leads us down a distracted path away from our purpose and destiny. To shake off our ashes, we must fix our eyes on the Author and Finisher of our faith. We must make space for God to breathe a simpler, more *authentic* hope into our hearts—a hope shaped by pure motives—a hope that leans upon a divine Source for its manifestation and fruition.

Hope

After walking through seasons of trial and test, we need to be attentive to the *real* needs and desires of our hearts—desires that for numerous reasons might seem unobtainable or beyond our reach. It's amazing how many aspirations we can come up with that are actually rooted in escapist mentality, insecurity, codependency, or other fear-driven motives, yet we cling to them as though they're our most earnest goals. When we fabricate dreams, our faith isn't fooled. Fraudulent hopes crafted out of desperation and confusion are like showy, shiny costumes made of slippery fabric. Clothing ourselves with these glitzy false hopes might help us to go on with the show, but real faith can only latch onto truth and divinely inspired vision.

Sometimes, when people are going through a tough season, they mistakenly interpret their difficult circumstances as a by-product of their own faithlessness. They struggle over a sense of failure, feeling ashamed, disqualified, and inadequate in their walk with God. The truth is, no matter how much faith we try to muster up, our hearts can still feel hurt, confused, paralyzed, and empty. Faith itself must have a true and reliable anchor from which to operate, and that anchor is hope. "Faith is the substance of things *hoped* for" (Hebrews 1:1, NKJV; italics mine). Faith is not the starting point for restoration in our lives, hope is. Faith flourishes where hope lives. When hope is alive, faith steps into action with ease.

When people have been through a furnace of affliction, whether sudden and unexpected or lengthy and slow burning, they often feel numb and dead inside. Genuine hope seems illusive, hard to cultivate, and no longer within their grasp. But Deuteronomy 30:14 (NIV) says, "The word is very near you; it is in your mouth and in your heart." As we draw close to the Savior and listen patiently for his voice, we *will* hear hope whispered into our wilting souls; our loving God will make sure of it.

Cover Up

I understand what it's like to feel completely devoid of hope. Suffering for years in an unhealthy marriage situation left me so devastated and so numb that my only hope was to someday have hope again. On the inside, my private, unseen, fiery trial had slowly and agonizingly burned me to a crisp, but on the outside, my ashes maintained the form of a happy woman leading a glamorous ministry life. I was struggling to hold together the ruins of my broken heart. I knew it was only a matter of time before an adverse wind would blow a little too hard upon my fragile substance, and those lifeless embers would be swept out of my hands. When that moment finally arrived, it was certainly no great surprise. Things had been heading in that direction for well over a decade.

It was difficult to accept what was happening. For the second time in my life, I felt completely and utterly hopeless. My strength was dried up and my soul was in fragments. As a minister and speaker, I was usually the one motivating others to stay strong and not give up the fight. Now it was *my* house of cards that was collapsing.

With the Christmas holiday season approaching, so also was my custom of establishing goals for the New Year—something my [former] husband and I usually did together. As I attempted to keep the annual ritual, I struggled to put pen to paper. I realized, in my grief, that for numerous years, many of the grandiose aspirations I had listed were, to some degree, a mask for the anguish I felt compelled to hide. They were a cover-up for my increasing sense of hopelessness over a desire for love and home—a reasonable longing that was growing more and more distant with each longsuffering year. These ministry aspirations, though genuine and inspired, were also a way to survive—a way to keep my head above water publicly while drowning in sorrow behind the scenes.

Breaking Point

What I needed was a true and genuine hope, a solid substance in which to anchor my faith. Despite years of enduring prayer, it seemed my one entirely worthwhile desire was impossible to attain. As the ball dropped in the Big Apple that New Year's Eve, it felt like critical mass in my soul.

I had stayed too long in a traumatizing situation that was eroding my well-being and sense of worth. The fabric of my soul was in ashes. I was fainting from fatigue and on the verge of collapse. I felt like I was standing on the edge of a high, steep cliff with my eyes facing the past and my back turned toward emptiness. I had no idea what the future held, but I knew God wanted me to let go of what I could not control and trust him to carry me to a safe haven. I knew he wanted me to free fall backwards into his everlasting arms. I had to believe he would catch me. I had to believe his arms were strong enough.

Carry You

I wrote a song during that hour of need to express the desperation I felt in my heart as well as the encouragement I received from the Savior. The song is titled "Carry You."

I see you hurting, lonely, and confused.
I hear you crying when you are abused.
I feel the sting of tears in your eyes,
pain with no disguise.
I've seen injustice and I know the taste,
broken hearts and trust that goes to waste.
I've felt betrayal and a lost embrace.
I've been in your place.
How I love you, how I love you.

Come on, just keep on believing,
fall right back into my arms,
and I will carry you.
Call, and I will come quickly.
You don't have to be so strong.
We're going to make it through.
I am going to carry you.

Pit of Despair

There's a time for all things, and it was time for me to let go of the broken pieces of my heart and entrust them into the loving hands of the Almighty. When I finally hit this breaking point, it was actually a macabre relief. It was in this vulnerable season that I began to discover Jesus in ways I'd never known him before. My discoveries were so beautiful that I've since become grateful for the pain that enlightened me to the Savior's consummate compassion.

One particularly memorable encounter took place during that desperate season of sadness. It was a time when tear-filled sunrises ran into fear-filled nights, and paralyzed weeks blurred into agonizing months. The hours seemed to pass in a fog during those days. It was as though my emotional and spiritual reservoir of strength was completely drained. Even if I'd wanted to keep serving and helping others, I couldn't. I was numb, broken, and hopeless. I told the Lord I'd decided on a plan of action from which I would not relent. In no uncertain terms, I informed him that I desired to climb down into a pit of despair and not come out—not for a long time. Choking out the words with tears streaming down my face, I reiterated my request out loud: "If it's okay with you, Jesus, I need to get down into a pit and not come out, not until I'm ready to—not for you, not for me, not for the ministry, not for my family, not for anyone."

With You

To my surprise, I heard an immediate response to my heart cry that changed my relationship with Jesus forever. He spoke to me tenderly with a depth of understanding that melted me to the core. "Of course, you can climb into a pit," he said. "And if it's okay with you, I'd like to get down in there with you and just hang out with you. And when you're ready, and only when you're ready, I'll climb out first, and then I'll help you climb out too."

Within the same instant, I "saw" my beloved, handsome Savior climb down into my dark bunker of sorrow. He sat down next to me and wrapped his arm around my shoulder to offer me comfort. He smiled at me warmly and leaned back against the wall. Then he lifted up his feet to casually rest them on the other side of my cramped cave. He looked peaceful, relaxed, and perfectly happy to be there. Without words, Jesus told me he understood what I was going through, and that he wanted me to be healed and strengthened. He made it clear that there was no rush and that he just wanted to be with me. I would have expected the King of kings to be standing on the edge of my pit, looking down impatiently, clicking his fingers, indicating it was time for me to get up and get out because there was kingdom work to be done, but no. No such thing. Not my Jesus.

The Jesus I Wish People Knew

Since that day, he is "the Jesus I wish people knew"—gracious, patient, deeply compassionate, and "intimately acquainted with all my ways" (Psalm 139: 3, NASB). His plan of action (from which he would not relent) was certainly not to push me or drive me. He understood that the pit I wanted to be in represented a refuge of escape from an agonizing ordeal. He had no intention of flippantly duct-taping my broken pieces back together again so I could rush back to being useful in his service as soon as possible. He saw how rundown I'd become in my damaging circumstances. *His* plan was to get me to a safe haven. *His* plan was for my *complete* restoration. *His* plan was to heal me, rebuild me, and make me new. My beloved Savior wanted to breathe hope into my heart again, and a dream that he could and would fulfill.

True, honest, and genuine restoration began when I sat down so Jesus could lift me up. It began with my surrender so he could be my victory. It began with my brokenness so he could be my wholeness. It began with my death so he could be my life. When Jesus sat down in my dark pit of despair, it was to be with me while I grieved my losses and shook off my ashes. For his acceptance of my humanness and utter concern for my brokenness, I am forever grateful.

Religion tells us that we need to hurry up and get our act together, but Jesus wants us to quit acting. I believe it saddens God to see his house run like a theater where no matter how wounded the cast might be, the show goes on. Though I wore my costume and mask for honorable reasons, playing a role like an actress in a play held me captive to a *form* of godliness that denied God's healing power and prevented me from taking stock of the very real dangers of my oppressive situation—a situation that needed intervention and heaven's hand of mercy.

Receiving confidential help and counsel at that time became the turning point in a situation that had already gone on far longer than it should have. I was presented with an opportunity to "sift my ashes" alongside a trustworthy friend and professional who could help me recognize what those ashes represented. When she affirmed that my circumstances warranted immediate change for the sake of my health and well-being, I was able to catch my first glimpse of light at the end of a very long and dark tunnel. John 1:5 (NLT) promises, "The light shines in the darkness, and the darkness can never extinguish it."

Choices

We all go through trials of one kind or another. Some are very severe. As we come out of each furnace of affliction, we must make a turning-point decision not to allow the lingering "smell of smoke" to remain woven into the fabric of our lives. We have a choice to make: We can either sit down in our ashes stoking yesterday's woes, convincing ourselves we have every right to do so after all we've been through, or we can allow ourselves to be rebuilt, and arise like a phoenix out of the fire.

We need to remember Shadrach, Meshach, and Abednego and their commendable attitudes after they came out of the furnace—how they wasted no time or energy fretting over King Nebuchadnezzar's injustice. Because of their no-fuss, courageous character, God's name was exalted in a land of idol worship and they were honored with promotion. I decided to follow their example and come out of my trials better off than I went in. The alternative was to have endured much but have little to show for it. I determined to learn from my experiences, shake off my ashes, and arise in my destiny and calling.

Sifting and Stoking

Learning from our trials is like sifting through ashes (perhaps in the same way articles of value might be retrieved from a burn site). It's an essential process on a journey of arising. Stoking, however, is not the same as sifting. Stoking is the prodding and reenactment of painful memories—the very thing that keeps us stuck in the past and smelling of smoke. The longer we stoke our memories, the more they keep smoldering. The more they keep smoldering, the "smellier" we become! Stoking our ashes through over-introspection perpetuates the negative beliefs and thought patterns formed amidst the confusion of our tests and trials. Reigniting memories by repeatedly dwelling on past pain slows our recovery. Granted, we may be frustrated that we're scarred so deeply we can barely recognize ourselves as the person we once were, but God's grace is sufficient and restoration is possible. We can be encouraged; our divine Physician is well able to erase our burn scars and re-sculpt us into a stronger, better, and more authentic version of who we are. I am living proof!

Once we've relinquished the "right" to stoke our ashes, we're ready to do the useful work of sifting. Sifting our ashes is the acknowledging, grieving, and accepting of the things that happened to us. It's also the nurturing of fresh trust in the here and now. It's the willingness to believe that our lives can be rebuilt into something beautiful, useful, and stable. It's the giving of permission for everything we experience to be used for the ultimate good. Having laid aside our fire pokers and having sifted our experiences with intentionality to learn valuable lessons, it's time to shake off our ashes.

Shaking Off and Letting Go

Shaking off our ashes starts with recognizing that they're there, and acknowledging that we've allowed them to accumulate and become part of our form. Whether it's lingering toxic tendencies, bitterness from accumulated hurts, broken self-imagery, numbed perspectives, or simply trying to be something we're not—shards such as these do not represent our true self. The fragmented parts of ourselves that paint on a smile for the crowd do not constitute our true substance— these ashes are an illusion of substance that we hold together for the sake of appearance. They no longer represent who we are. They no longer represent our lives in the present. It's crucial we stop holding onto the ashes of our past in the hope of making them the substance of our future. Reaching the end of our own strength, or the end of a relationship or season can be a golden opportunity to let go of the things that no longer play a role in the next stage of our destiny. It's a chance to be rebuilt from the inside out with solid, "fireproof" materials. When it comes to arising, it makes little sense to sit in the toxic fallout of yesterday's fiery furnace when we can flourish in a hope-filled future and a glorious new now. Even so, shaking off our ashes can seem difficult simply because those ashes are familiar to us. Letting go of familiar things can feel risky, even if they represent destructive or negative forces in our lives.

God, however, is the solid rock upon which we can stand assured. Life may not feel or be risk free, but unconditional love is. Fiery trials and internal infernos can level us to rock bottom, but when they do, we have an opportunity to rebuild our lives upon things that are unshakable. Turmoil and shaking can be useful gifts that help us to rightly divide true substance from flaky, reliable from insecure, real from fake, and valuable from worthless. Letting go is a decision. Regardless of how precarious it might feel to say good-bye to the familiarity of the past, if it's toxic it has to go!

Fragments and Broken Pieces

Whether it's our own negative patterns, a damaging relationship, an outgrown season, or a broken situation, at the juncture of letting go, we can find ourselves paralyzed in time, afraid to unwrap our frightened fingers from the frail yet familiar fragments of our lives. We fear there might be nothing left of us if we do. But grasping ashes is a futile endeavor. Holding onto broken pieces only prolongs our injury. Closing our hands tightly around false hopes that are certain to disappoint is masochistic at best and insanity at worst. Our loving Savior understands that we might feel scared or stricken, but he encourages us to trust him all the same.

After miraculously feeding over five thousand people with a few loaves and fish, Jesus instructed his disciples to "gather up the fragments that remain, that nothing be lost" (John 6:12, KJV). If the Messiah was concerned about fragments of *bread* being lost, we can certainly rest assured that he's watching over the fragments of our lives with the utmost concern.

We may feel fragmented by our ordeals, but peace comes from knowing that our Savior desires to gather up all our broken pieces—emotional, spiritual, mental, and physical. He wants us to be assured that no part of us will be forgotten, wasted, or abandoned. Our heavenly Father wants to gather us up in his arms and take care of us. He has an awesome plan for our lives and he fully intends to see that it's fulfilled. God is the master craftsman. Like paint to an artist and clay to a potter, the fragments of our lives in God's loving hands will become an extraordinary masterpiece.

Earthquakes and Aftershocks

In the 1990s, I experienced firsthand the 5.7 earthquake that affected Northridge, California, and the surrounding areas. My memory of it still remains clear to this day. It was about five o'clock in the morning when I was shaken from sleep by gut churning rumbles emanating from the depths of the earth. The steady ground I was accustomed to standing on suddenly became fragile and untrustworthy. I stumbled to the crib of my firstborn son, anxious to hold him close and protect him from harm. With both arms wrapped around my precious little bundle, it was a struggle to keep from falling down. Standing under the frame of the bedroom door, I watched our apartment sway and tilt before my eyes. The chandelier swung, the bookshelves toppled, cans and jars fell off the pantry shelves. I held my breath for what seemed like an hour, all the while bracing myself as the foundation of the building rippled and rolled under my feet. It was an unforgettable experience. All I hoped for in those moments was that we would survive to tell the tale.

Physical earthquakes are traumatizing enough, but *emotional* earthquakes can be even more harrowing. Circumstances upon which we once stood firm can suddenly feel like crushed glass beneath our feet. Life, that at one point seemed stable, can suddenly feel like a high wire act in a hurricane. Like physical earthquakes, internal earthquakes can leave us feeling so disheveled and tossed to and fro that our hope is simply to survive the ride!

When the shaking of the Los Angeles earthquake finally stopped, people stood dumbfounded and shocked. Aside from the time-consuming process of sorting through the debris of damaged possessions, it took weeks to process the internal stress generated by the event. The aftershocks were almost as unnerving as the earthquake itself. When a tremor hit, I found myself bracing to endure the experience all over again even though an earthquake wasn't actually happening.

Situations resembling unpleasant scenarios from the past are like earthquake aftershocks. When they come our way, we tend to brace ourselves as though a reenactment of those experiences is taking place once again. This is the body's natural way of dealing with trauma; self-protection kicks in when there appears to be a threat. Even so, continual negative reactions based on memories of unpleasant experiences are like smoke arising from re-stoked ashes. These old reaction patterns don't belong in our new present. Self-defensive responses based on projected preconceptions can make our lives feel like a perpetual emotional earthquake. Living this way can leave us stuck in the past and disconnected from the glorious potential of each new moment.

Even though we may have done our best to let go of the past, there'll be times when we will feel as though it has not let go of us. In such instances, we must be quick to differentiate between our true, current reality and the deceptive delusions of "circumstantial aftershocks." Even though the Bible assures us: "The old things passed away; behold, new things have come" (2 Corinthians 5:17, NASB), we must partner with God to reprogram the "default operating system" in our subconscious that can be quick to interpret circumstantial aftershocks as circumstantial earthquakes. We do this by intentionally and repeatedly aligning our perspectives with the security that is ours in the Savior's love, and with the truth that we cannot control what happens outside of ourselves, but we *can* control how we respond to it.

Ground Zero

The Northridge earthquake left millions of dollars of structural damage in its wake. In numerous cases, cosmetic touch ups weren't enough for the substantial repair that was needed. Many buildings had to be gutted and renovated. At times, we might feel like our life resembles a construction zone. Even the very foundation of our beliefs might need to be re-laid.

Shaking off our ashes involves just that—a shaking. Though difficult to endure, the only way to move forward in genuine faith is through "the removing of what can be shaken... so that what cannot be shaken may remain" (Hebrews 12:27, NIV). When my world felt like it collapsed and my existence felt like ground zero, God whispered this hope into my heart: "I will build you and you will be rebuilt" (Jeremiah 31:4, NASB). I'm grateful to tell you, my loving Savior has been faithful to keep that promise, and I know he will do the same for you too.

Truth be told, the rebuilding process often felt like it was more than I could handle. It took many challenging years living in the daily discomfort of internal renovation and reconstruction to accomplish such a deep healing work, but the restoration of my soul was worth every difficult moment. A heaven-sent shaking can be scary and unpleasant. It can leave us feeling more vulnerable and fragile than we've ever felt before, but it's a necessary step if we want to accurately appraise the true substance of our lives and build a future that is solid and unshakable.

A Divine Exchange

When I climbed down into my pit of despair, it was partly to grieve what could have been and should have been but wasn't. I cried many tears at that time. Those tears served to soften the scabs of confusion and hopelessness that clung so steadfastly to my soul. The rainfall of my sorrow irrigated the ravaged soil of my heart making it ready for true restoration and seeds of fresh hope. As I prepared to embrace a new season, I sifted the ashes of my past to glean insight and wisdom from all that I'd been through. Then, I shook those ashes off, and laid them to rest for good.

Whether in severe fiery trials or daily life, the heat of the battle can get intense; it's understandable that we get burned out from time to time. Shaking off ashes needs to become a regular practice if we want to smell sweet and smoke free. A regular dusting off also helps prevent accumulated ashes from crusting over and hardening our hearts.

The time to make a divine exchange is upon us. God promises us a crown of beauty instead of ashes, the oil of joy instead of mourning, and a garment of praise to replace despair. As we exchange the ashes of our past for new perspectives and new hope, we'll be challenged to redefine who we are based on the *true substance* that remains after the fire. A season of redefining and rebuilding isn't always comfortable, but it's better for us to be temporarily razed to the ground and rebuilt with fireproof materials than to be an illusion of substance made from yesterday's ashes.

It's time for us to shake off our ashes and allow the lingering smell of smoke from our furnaces of affliction to be washed away forever. Then, the sweet fragrance of the Savior will rest upon us and saturate our being. The past will become a distant memory, and it will truly be a new day. God has given us his word: "I am about to do something new. See, I have already begun!" (Isaiah 43:19, NLT)

It is time to arise.

It is time to shake off your ashes.

Reflections

3
Know Your Value

Choices

I lost my virginity as a teenager to a boy whose name I can't remember and whose face I can't recall. It was an unpleasant experience born more out of curiosity than attraction. I didn't love him, and he didn't love me. In fact, we hardly knew each other. We probably recognized that our daring adventure was wrong on every level, but for whatever reason at the time, we didn't care.

I still cringe over certain memories from my younger days and the numerous self-demeaning choices that I made. Like so many teenagers, I had little understanding of my own value and worth. Consequently, I established few, if any, boundaries to my heart. I simply wasn't aware there was anything of great value to guard or protect—an oversight that led to a struggle with low self-esteem for much of my young adulthood.

Identity Crisis

In sharing this memory, I'm certainly not making light of the pitfalls of promiscuity. On the contrary, I'm shedding light on this morally ignoble element of my past as an example of the downward spiral that can so easily develop from a deeper root issue. And it is this issue that plagues humanity at large. It is the very thing that causes us to miss the mark of our potential on every level.

In my particular case, I can say it this way: The originator of my self-depreciating choices and derailed self-esteem was a disconnection from my true identity. My erroneous lifestyle evolved from the absence of a stable root by which I could establish a sense of confidence, purpose, and worth. Simply put, I had no idea who I was.

Too few of us understand our true value—either to God, to the planet, or to humanity. As a result, a sense of aimlessness, "homelessness," and disconnection pervades the hearts and minds of millions. Worst still, codependency has become a virtual epidemic in our world today. As human beings, we're wired for connection, but entering relationships in an attempt to fill a void, secure one's identity, or establish a sense of personal value is a futile endeavor, of course. Even so, it happens often. Such symbiotic behavior is not limited to personal relationships either. Codependent or dysfunctional tendencies can show up in our parenting, professional lives, hobbies, and religious activities—even our self-improvement efforts. Seeking to establish our security, happiness, and personal worth through a person, activity, or thing will leave us empty-handed every time. But as long as we remain unclear about our true identity and worth, we'll keep coming back for more, even if our perceived source of fulfillment fails to satisfy.

In the western society workforce, "soul prostitution" is rampant. The temptation to sell one's soul for fifteen minutes of fame is surprisingly powerful. Climbing corporate ladders of success and achievement might *appear* to offer the much-craved esteem we long for, but the unhealthy output so often required in "reaching the top" can damage our ability to ascertain our own inherent value and uniqueness. As a result, too many people become stuck in the mire of occupational co-dependency or dysfunction, bled dry for every drop of productivity they can offer, but at significant personal cost.

Influential Experiences

In addition to carrying co-dependent tendencies into the work place and relationships, it's not unusual for people to carry heart dysfunction into a relationship with God as well. People have a tendency to form their beliefs about God and about life through their personal experiences at an early age, especially with authority figures and relationships of influence. Negative or positive, these influential experiences contribute greatly toward the sculpting of internal value systems and core beliefs.

Beliefs about God cultivated out of troubled memories or painful experiences can leave us distanced from, or unaware of, God's unconditional love for us. Painful experiences of rejection and abandonment can build subconscious walls deep within our souls that make it difficult for us to receive that unconditional love. In my own experience, having been rejected and forsaken by the love of my life, it took a while for my subconscious soul to lay hold of promises such as "I will never leave you nor forsake you," (Hebrews 13:5, ESV) and "I am with you always, even to the end of the age" (Matthew 28:20, NLT).

God Chooses, Not Uses

When we struggle to receive God's unconditional love, we become susceptible to the idea that our value and identity are based on what we do rather than who we are. These deep-rooted inclinations can spill over into all manners of activities—even the work of the ministry.

I always feel a little uneasy when I hear people say, "God wants to *use* you," or "God wants to *use* your life for his purposes." (This term has certainly become a kingdom catch phrase, yet to this day, I have not found it anywhere in the Bible.) I understand the sincerity behind the lingo, but we must be careful not to insinuate that God is a user who's more interested in our talents than our friendship. God doesn't use us, he *chooses* us. He saves us, redeems us, and lifts us up to sit beside him. He invites us to *partner* with him in the building of his kingdom. All the while, he lavishes his love upon us, even into eternity. It's imperative we be grounded in this one truth: If we did nothing more for God for the rest of our lives, he would love us unconditionally just the same.

The idea that God *uses* people is a contradiction to his character. Users are selfish; their motives are typically self-satisfying. They're not concerned with the well-being and safety of the person being used. A user mentality is entirely contrary to God's trustworthy and gracious heart. God desires that we do things for him and for others out of a free will and a pure heart. He wants our service for him to be motivated by love, not fear, insecurity, or obligation. God values us deeply and he will never abuse, invalidate, or exploit our freewill at any time.

Ephesians 1:4 (NLT) says, "Even before he made the world, God loved us and chose us." God isn't watching for a perfect performance. He doesn't exploit his "best people" on a kingdom ministry playing field and bench those who don't make the grade. We're chosen for a specific purpose: to be loved and cherished, now and forever. Each and every one of us is a perfect candidate for that love. There are no exceptions.

Unchangeable Truth

Throughout the four Gospels of the New Testament, we're given an opportunity to take a closer look at the loving, kind, and compassionate nature of God. The Son of God lived as a man to model and represent God's character. Jesus is described as being "the exact representation of his nature" (Hebrews 1:3, NASB). He said, "He who has seen me has seen the Father" (John 14:9, NKJV). Jesus came to show mankind what God is like so we wouldn't confuse his perfect, sinless character with man's imperfect, iniquitous character.

Most of us have heard it said that God is loving and good, and most of us have the capacity to believe it. Yet all too often, we find ourselves living at a distance from our Savior's all-inclusive provision, far below our redeemed stature. The problem is this: even if we *believe* in God's goodness, we might struggle to see ourselves as a worthy recipient of it. As a result, our trust and faith toward the Savior can become inconsistent. An unhealthy combination of calm and chaos might ebb and flow in our hearts. We might be up in the clouds singing God's praises one minute, but weighed down by shame and fear the next. If our sense of identity is vague and uncertain, we'll be subject to a storm-tossed existence in which external circumstances dictate our perspectives, responses, and decisions.

Our sense of worth and identity must be rooted in unchangeable truth, not in the everchanging tide of our relationships and circumstances. It's time for us to know our value. But where do we start in this seemingly complex process of knowing who we are? I believe the best place to start is in the beginning—literally, the origin of mankind.

In the Beginning

In the beginning, Adam and Eve walked and talked with God in the Garden of Eden. There in that garden paradise, they enjoyed the beauty of creation and the experience of intrinsic divinity. It was the perfect life. Genesis 2:25 (NIV) says "they felt no shame." Stress, anguish, and hurt weren't in the picture. Guilt and sadness were nowhere to be found. The concepts of esteem and worth didn't exist because man was in unity with himself and with God. He was fully conscious of his value and completeness—in fact, he knew no other way to be. He experienced faultless fulfillment, perfect peace, and unhindered harmony.

For most of us, that kind of internal tranquility seems like a distant ideal, yet it has *always* been God's intention for mankind to live that way. Even if we don't taste the paradise of spiritual oneness and connection with God in this lifetime, we *will* do so in heaven for all eternity. But if we're to apply the redemptive work of Christ to our lives on earth and make steps toward living in the completeness that's been restored to us, it's crucial we understand three things: (1) Our origin, life source, substance, and essence, (2) An understanding of what The Tree of the Knowledge of Good and Evil represents, and (3)

An understanding of the gift of redemption.

Origin and Substance

Genesis, the book of origins, describes how God created all living things by speaking to the substance of its derivation or sustenance. For example, when God created the plants and vegetation, he addressed the earth: "*Let the earth* sprout vegetation" (Genesis 1:11, NASB). When God created the creatures of the sea, he addressed the waters: "*Let the waters* teem with living creatures" (Genesis 1:20, NASB). When God created the animals, again he spoke to the earth saying, "*Let the earth* bring forth living creatures after their kind" (Genesis 1:24, NASB; italics mine).

Understanding that God created all living things by speaking to the substance of its derivation or sustenance is crucially important, because only when living things are *connected* to that substance do they have the potential for life. When they are not connected to the substance of their derivation and sustenance, sooner or later, they die.

This truth becomes even more important as we look at the origin of mankind. When God made man, he didn't speak to the waters and he didn't speak to the earth. To create man, God did just as he did when he created all other living things: he spoke to the very substance and essence out of which man is derived and sustained. The following statement and scripture, therefore, become potentially life-changing in the light of these scriptural facts: When God created man, he spoke *to himself* saying, "Let us make mankind in our image, in our likeness" (Genesis 1:26, NIV; italics mine). This God did on the sixth day of creation as recorded in Genesis chapter one.

Think about what this implies. When God created man, he spoke to himself. Therefore, the origin, essence, and sustenance of mankind is God. Whether or not we understand it completely, we're made of

"God stuff." Our identity is established upon this key truth: We're the offspring of the omnipotent, eternal Spirit. We are *of* God, *like* God, and *made of* God substance. Our lives have unspeakable value.

Earthsuit

We see that the forming of man's body out of the earth is recorded a little later in scripture, in Genesis chapter two. Man's body, or earth suit (as I like to call it), is the temporary housing for his *spirit*—the very substance that was born out of God himself. After our earth suits stop functioning, they return back to the earth from which they were formed. But the creatively powerful spirit inside our bodies is *not* made of earthly material. It is made of "God material." The Spirit of God is eternal and abides forever. Therefore, so do we.

Grasping this incredible and life-changing truth is crucial to establishing our value and identity. We're not born just to strive and survive. We're more than a random conglomeration of thoughts and emotions housed in an "earth suit." We have an origin, a home, a spiritual birthplace, and a divine life Source. We're eternal spirits housed in male and female forms so as to fully represent the attributes of God. We are man and "womb-man" derived from God in the likeness and image of God. "Likeness" in the original Hebrew is *d'mwuth*—pronounced demooth—meaning "resemblance, similitude, comparable."

Home Turf

Understanding the significance of our origin and God-substance is an important element to arising and living in the fullness of our potential. Plants and animals cannot live up to their potential separated from the earth, the substance of their derivation. Sea creatures cannot live up to their potential separated from the water, the habitat from which they were called into being. In the same way, we cannot live in the fullness of *our* potential—the quality of life intended for us from the beginning—if we are separated or estranged from the life Source from which we're derived. It makes sense that the first words I heard God speak to my heart were, "It's alright, Michele. You're home now, you're home." Like a tender flower plucked from the earth, I was withered and dying, disconnected from my sustenance and place of origin. I needed to get home. I needed to get permanently re-housed in the Spirit of God—the only Source by which I, or any of us, can flourish and grow. God, the divine Spirit, the Source of all life and love, is the habitat in which we flourish. God is our home turf.

Death

Having uncovered the life-changing truth of man's substance, derivation, and Source of life, we need to understand what caused the separation between mankind and God and the departure of man from his home in the Garden of Eden.

We know that in the beginning, Adam and Eve communed with God in fulfillment, completeness, and contentment. They were oblivious to the concepts of worth, anxiety, lack, and shame. Such things did not exist in their realm of understanding because they lived in the antithesis of a negative self-conscious state.

We also know that Satan (in the form of a serpent) deceived Adam and Eve into disobeying and disregarding a crucial instruction and warning from God: "You must not eat from the tree of the knowledge of good and evil, for when you eat from it you will certainly die" (Genesis 2:17, NIV). (The word *die* here in Hebrew is *muwth*—pronounced mooth—and is of the same word family as *d'muwth*, meaning "likeness" that we looked at earlier. *Muwth* means "die, kill, destroy, not wise." It's a word associated with the idea of being *worthy of death*.)

"But the serpent said to the woman, 'You will not surely die. For God knows that when you eat of it your eyes will be opened, and you will be like God...'" (Genesis 3:4, 5, ESV).

Truth versus Doubt

We need to understand the incredible significance of God's instruction, Satan's deception, and the subsequent consequence of eating the fruit of the Tree of the Knowledge of Good and Evil. Understanding what this inauspicious tree and its fruit represent is crucial to the restoration of our communion with God and our full comprehension of Christ's eternal gift of redemption (described in greater detail later this chapter).

To eat the fruit of the Tree of the Knowledge of Good and Evil is to feed on doubt with regards to our completeness, similitude, and right standing with God. It is to feed on a mindset of lack. Lack— deficiency, incompleteness, and the absence of what we need and desire—is the exact opposite of what man was created to experience. Satan knew if he could deceive mankind into believing that he was incomplete and not enough—if he could get him to believe that he needed to be more, do more, know more, and get more—this lie, this exact opposite of God's already established position and intention for man would separate him from God.

Satan's goal was to persuade man to feed on the idea that he was inadequate—that he needed to be *like God*. He knew if mankind fell for that lie, he would bite into the antithesis of life and become disconnected from who he *already was*—made in God's likeness. He would become separated from his peace-filled, love-filled, perfect completeness. He would become disconnected from his own powerful potential and the truth of who he really is! He would become like a house divided against itself—a vessel of death *and* life, fear *and* love, strife *and* contentment.

Death versus Likeness

We have learned that the Hebrew word for likeness is *d'muwth*, meaning "comparable, similar." We have also learned that the Hebrew word for death is *muwth*, meaning "die, kill, destroy, not wise"—a word associated with being worthy of death and anything that pertains to death. In a nutshell summary, we can put it like this: *We experience death (and a sense that we're worthy of death) when we lose connection with who we really are in essence and likeness to God.* This happens both in the literal sense of physical death, as well as in a diminished sense of worth, purpose, and vitality.

After Adam and Eve disobeyed God's wise command and ate the fruit of the Tree of the Knowledge of Good and Evil, God asked the question, "Where are you?" (Genesis 3:9, NIV) This indicated that man had entered a realm of existence that God could not relate to, for "God is light; in him there is no darkness at all" (1 John 1:5, NIV). Separation had occurred between man and God. A veil of unbelief had fallen between them.

We are not God. We never will be and wouldn't want to be; that was Satan's rebellious and wicked desire. But being comparable to God in substance and essence is what opens the way for communion and partnership—something God longs for and one of the chief purposes for which we were brought into being. Our understanding of this truth is essential if we're to embrace Christ's redemption and benefit from the fullness of all that's been accomplished for us by the Savior.

Man's separation from God (often referred to as the "fall of man") is typically attributed to man's rebellion. But I would like to suggest that this sin nature, this "missing the mark," did not come about because man was "intrinsically bad." (On the contrary, Genesis 1:31

(NIV) declares that, "God saw all that he made, and it was very good.") It came about because the first woman and the first man allowed themselves to be deceived into believing they were not enough— not truly consummated in God's likeness. It was this wayward belief, contrary to Adam and Eve's God-given perfection, that led to their separation from home, Father, and the Tree of Life.

Jesus states Satan's universal mission in John 10:10 (BSB): "The thief comes only to steal and kill and destroy. I have come that they may have life, and have it in all its fullness." In making this statement, Jesus was mindful of man's fall in the Garden of Eden. He was declaring his original intention for man: life that is abundant in every way. And he was reminding us how that quality of life was stolen from us to begin with.

Shame

The mission of the "the thief" has always been the same: 1) To *destroy* our correct perception of who we are: complete in God (Colossians 2:10, KJV). 2) To *steal* our confidence and identity as God's offspring: comparable, similar, and made in his likeness (Genesis 1:26, NASB). 3) To *kill* us little by little (even through religion) through the idea that we're worthy of the effects of death, unworthy of abundant life, and that we must labor for our right standing with God.

It's no surprise that the first feeling Adam and Eve experienced after eating the prohibited fruit was that of incompleteness—nakedness—a sense that they needed to cover up their inadequacy and make up for what was missing. They had eaten the fruit of unbelief concerning their likeness to God and their union with him. They now considered themselves "less than" and felt compelled to hide from their Father— the one with whom they had previously felt a sense of perfect peace and belonging. Their bodies (earth suits) still functioned, but the substance of their identity was now poisoned with self-doubt. This poison was already making its way through their bodies and souls to bring about "*mwuth*" rather than "*d'mwuth*"—death (and its separating consequences) rather than similitude and connection with God. By ingesting the poison of doubt about who they were as the offspring of God, and swallowing the lie that satisfaction could only be derived from something outside of themselves, they literally fed on self-damnation; they literally destroyed themselves.

Lies

The fall of man can be summed up in this one profound statement: *In attempting to fill a void within themselves that didn't actually exist, Adam and Eve created one.* The day of man's fall in the Garden of Eden was Satan's victorious "opposite day." Satan had promised Adam and Eve that their eyes would be opened. But of course, the father of lies speaks *lies*. Their eyes were now actually *blinded* to who they were; they could no longer see themselves in their true image and identity. Satan had promised they would be like God. But of course, that was a trick. *Before* Adam and Eve ate the fruit of self-doubt from the Tree of the Knowledge of Good and Evil, they *were* like God— made in his image and likeness—confident, fulfilled, and lacking nothing. But once they ingested the lie that they could and should be more like God, the poison of that very desire took up residence in their cells.

In their blinded, usurped, displaced condition Adam and Eve were no longer in harmony with their paradisiacal home and surroundings. (It's likely they felt they no longer belonged there.) It is for this reason, the omniscient God called to Adam asking, "Where are you?" (Genesis 3:9, NIV) For the man and woman now lived in a state of existence that was foreign to their Father. God knew if they ate from the Tree of Life they would be eternally incarcerated to their deceived condition with no hope of rescue. And so the first man and the first woman were evicted from the Garden of Eden.

Only Redemption

Since that day, mankind has been born with an inherent sin nature—a nature that's missing the mark, disconnected from his infinite potential and his perfect and shameless union with God. But God's plan is for us to arise—to be born again and come into being—to live in the fullness of abundant life and all that was intended for us from the beginning.

On our planet, at this time in history, there's an awakening that's taking place through many spiritual movements, irreligious or otherwise. It's an emergence of souls who are intuitively tuning in to an awareness of their God essence and likeness, and the original intention for mankind to be partners and co-creators with Source energy. Many of these movements encourage their followers to re-attain their divine status and union with God though mental assertion. (This is comparable, perhaps, to the modern-day building of a psychological Tower of Babel.) But thanks be to God, through Christ's redeeming sacrifice, we are gifted with God's own perfect righteousness and everlasting life. "The payment for sin is death, but the gift that God freely gives is everlasting life found in Christ Jesus" (Romans 6:23, GWT). "God sent his Son to have a human nature as sinners have and to pay for sin. That way, God condemned sin in our corrupt nature" (Romans 8:3, GWT). "Our old sinful selves were crucified with Christ so that sin might lose its power in our lives" (Romans 6:6, NLT). "By that one offering he forever made perfect those who are being made holy" (Hebrews 10:14, NLT).

Jesus accomplished for us that which is impossible for us to accomplish through our own efforts. Only redemption can bring us back to our intended place of communion and connection with God, with each other, and with ourselves. The Son of God gave his life to pay for that redemption. He now invites us to receive his goodness without labor, strife, or doubt. By sacrificing his own life for us, Jesus negated the lie that we're worthy of death. He cancelled out our "not enough" by restoring back to us everything we lost.

Stay Connected

Now that we understand our true identity, and the means by which it is so easily stolen from us, we can understand why Jesus had harsh words for the Pharisees who aggressively propagated the idea that man must religiously strive for his right standing with God. We can also begin to grasp the magnitude of redemption, how impossible it is for us to attain it by our own efforts, and the reason why Jesus said, "This is the only work God wants from you: Believe in the one he has sent" (John 6:29, NLT).

Jesus became sin for us "that we might become God's righteousness in him" (2 Corinthians 5:21, Darby Bible Translation). We cannot add to or subtract from the completeness to which we've now been restored through the perfect redemptive work of Christ. To do so would be to swallow the same lie that Adam and Eve swallowed in the Garden— the lie that they needed to *do more* so they could *be more*—the lie that they must strive by their own works to be good enough to attain right standing with God when it was already theirs to enjoy!

Through Christ's sacrificial death, identity theft has been reversed. Mankind can now be reconnected to himself and to the Source of his origin in the truth: "You are complete in him" (Colossians 2:10, KJV) and "In him you have redemption" (Ephesians 1:7 NIV). This really leaves man with only one specific need. When that one need is met, every other need can be successfully met too.

What is man's one need? To stay connected to his Source. Jesus said, "Live in me, and I will live in you. A branch cannot produce any fruit by itself. It has to stay attached to the vine. In the same way, you cannot produce fruit unless you live in me" (John 15:4, GWT).

Rooted in Love

1 John 4:8 (NIV) tells us "God is love." When we're replanted in the home turf of our spiritual derivation and substance, and reconnected to the Source that meets our every need, we become rooted in God—rooted in unconditional love. We then have the potential for God's unconditional love to flow to us, in us, and through us at all times. This eliminates our misperceived need for codependent and dysfunctional relationships as a means by which to obtain a sense of value and security.

It's important we understand that people can offer us love, nurture, care, compassion, help, strength, knowledge, guidance, and so much more, but they can never be the *source* of these things for us. People can be vessels through which these godly characteristics might be displayed or shared, but they themselves are not the limitless, infallible, and reliable wellspring from which they originate. We can feel at home with certain people, but they can never serve as our essential life-giving habitat. We can live alongside people in a marriage, relationship, tribe, friendship, business, or family, but ultimately, people cannot be our security, provision, or eternal safety. It's our individual responsibility to be connected to the one and only reliable Source of everlasting and unconditional love—the Source of our sustenance by which we become established in our own unshakable identity and worth.

Looking for Love in All the Wrong Places

Everything we have need of has been provided. Yet our contrary, subconscious core beliefs and our blindness to redemption's life-changing power keep us from the unconditional love we crave. No wonder Paul prayed that the eyes of our hearts would be enlightened, so we would know the hope of his calling. (Ephesians 1:18)

We're designed to experience unconditional love, so it's understandable that we seek after it. The problem comes when we look for love in the wrong places and interpret our inevitable lack of success as a reason to feel worthless. In my teenage years, when I was disconnected from my value and identity, I put myself out on the market of relationships with few, if any, boundaries. In my desire to feel valued, I figured any attention was good attention. In my subconscious belief system, I equated attention with approval and approval with love. In a world of bargain hunters looking for a good deal, I put myself up for keeps like a reduced item on a clearance aisle.

New Creation

Once Jesus came into my life, you'd have thought my Cinderella-in-rags story would have come to a close. After being found and chosen wasn't Cinderella supposed to leave behind her slavish lifestyle? Wasn't she supposed to take her glorious place beside her powerful prince and fully embrace the fullness of restoration? No question about it; that *is* Jesus's plan for the bedraggled souls who enter into his magnificent kingdom. Rescue and redemption were fully available to me from the moment I asked Jesus to make me new, but the suffocating chokehold of a self-depreciating belief system prevented me from enjoying the freedom that had become mine.

When I asked Jesus to save me, he didn't patch up my former self, he made me a brand-new creation. It was as though I'd been given a born-again birthday gift in the form of a "spiritual check." In the amount space was written: "blessed with every spiritual blessing" (Ephesians

1:3, NASB) and "all things that pertain to life and godliness" (2 Peter 1:3, NASB). Eternally speaking, I was saved from death. Spiritually speaking, I was reconnected to unlimited power and unconditional love. Yet an understanding of my spiritual derivation and worth still eluded me. My eyes needed to be opened, and my mind needed to be renewed so that I could confidently tap into all that was available to me. God had given me a spiritual heritage of incalculable worth. Now he wanted me to enjoy the benefits of that heritage.

The Early Years

On the most part, my growing up years were good. My dad worked hard and my mum was always there for me. Like most couples, my parents had their problems, but they remained together and provided a stable home. I adored my older brother; he was, and still is, an inspiration to me. My sensitive, compliant personality, however, often made me a gullible target for his big brother antics and practical jokes. He remembers these "games" as playful, but I remember them as tormenting. When he bullied me, he was smart to keep it behind closed doors. Consequently, my parents didn't always take me seriously when I appealed to them for protection. This left me feeling vulnerable as a little girl—a feeling that continued on into my adult life.

My father, an articulate and talented artist whom I love and admire dearly, was unfortunately given to outbursts of anger when displeased. These frightening interludes were so disturbing to me that I learned at an early age to do whatever was needed to keep the peace. I remember one incident with particular clarity; it happened when I was eight years old.

Lesson Learned

Late one night, my brother repeatedly called upon me to adjust the placement of his bedroom door. To him, it was just a game, but I was the one being "played." Over and over, I climbed in and out of bed to painstakingly adjust his door as commanded, and gleefully, he took full advantage of my gullible sweetness. After about an hour, I snapped. In my frustration and weariness, I called him a bad name. (It was a word I'd heard in school the week before but didn't know the meaning of.) Before I knew what was happening, my brother was racing downstairs to snitch on me for using bad language.

The outcome was ugly, but it wasn't untypical. My dad ran up the stairs and burst into my bedroom. Unbeknownst to him in the dimness and circumstantial discord, I wasn't fully dressed at the time. Without stopping to hear my side of the tale, he spanked me harshly. The seemingly unfair action left me feeling physically sore and deeply shamed. No doubt he believed he was doing his duty as a parent to reprimand me for using a bad word, but the incident left me with an internal scar for years to come. In fact, it stands out to me as one of the worst memories of my childhood. That night, it was as though I had "learned my lesson well" as the series of similar experiences quietly endured during my girlhood years culminated in an internal resolve: If I wanted to feel safe around men, gain their approval and acceptance, and lay my head down on my pillow at night in peace, I would have to do whatever they required of me regardless of the humiliation or discomfort I might suffer. I can still remember standing bedside my bed with tears streaming down my face, making a vow in my heart (and therefore, in my subconscious). The vow was this: "I must do whatever it takes to keep men happy in order to avoid their anger or rejection, even if I become degraded or devalued in the process."

Dealing with the Root

Looking back, it's obvious to me now that I developed an expectation for people to show indifference or disregard for my feelings. In fact, for several decades as an adult, I allowed myself to remain in a situation in which I tolerated abuse and coercion. I suffered much stress and trauma as a result of those years. No doubt such patterns were intrinsically linked to the inner vows I made in my childhood and to the self-depreciating core beliefs that were formed in my subconscious as a result.

Most of us probably suffered some kind of bullying, abuse, or struggle in our formative years. Some people's upbringings are so horrific, my little story sounds like a cheery fairy tale in comparison. The details of our wounding experiences can vary greatly, but the outcome typically does not. Regardless of the type or severity of our traumatic experiences, we tend to form core beliefs in the midst of those experiences that can mold our personalities and drive our thought processes for years to come. These patterns of thought can become deeply sculpted within our subconscious souls. In fact, they have the potential to become the "default operating system" by which our entire lives are run, played out through dysfunctional symptoms in our relationships and day-to-day choices.

The dysfunctional symptoms in our lives, therefore, are the clues that lead us to the root of our problems. And it's the root we need to work on, not just the fruit. These root problems can be difficult to decipher and even harder to face, but if we truly desire to arise in our maximum potential and become the best version of ourselves we can be, they must be addressed. We must be willing to go beyond behavior management as a temporary solution for our dysfunction. If we want to experience lasting, internal transformation, we must identify unhealthy roots and realign our core beliefs to the truth of our value and identity.

Crash and Burn

In addition to my skewed sense of self-worth, I was also plagued with a fear of material lack for the first few decades of my life. I remember many Friday mornings as a preschooler being asked by my mother to hide from the milkman when he came to collect. The fact that we consistently struggled to come up with the one pound, fifty pence to pay to the milk bill downloaded the message "there isn't enough" into my subconscious self at an early age. Anyone raised in a financially insecure environment can probably relate.

The deep-rooted fear of lack that grew up out of that subconscious core belief drove me to work long hours and always keep a second job. My mission: to store up money for the day my income would cease and the bottom would fall out from beneath my career. I literally behaved as though such an outcome were inevitable.

I was especially certain this would be the case because the lofty performance standards I set for myself were so high and so exhausting they were almost impossible to maintain. Deep down in my heart, I believed it was only a matter of time before I would crash and burn.

My work was very physical. For many years, I spent seven or eight hours a day dancing full out as a professional dancer, choreographer, or teacher. When it came to teaching, "average" was never an option; I wanted the job done right, so I taught everything by demonstration. The continual physical output was daunting and draining. I was weary beyond words, but I wouldn't stop. There was another root driving all of this frantic activity: an obsession with staying thin.

Numbers

I was first required to watch my weight when I was eleven years old. As a gymnast in consideration for the national team, staying thin was everything. I made the A Squad at the age of thirteen, which meant I was one of the top twenty-four gymnasts in Britain at that time. Shortly after taking my place on the British team, however, puberty kicked in. I felt obliged to my parents (who paid for all my training and competition expenses) to sidestep this unwanted growth spurt at all costs. I knew that puberty would cause me to gain weight, and gaining weight would prevent me from pulling off the high scoring skills that kept me on the medal stand. This would result in expulsion from the team—something I needed to avoid at all costs. I feared my father's disapproval intensely; in fact, it was the driving force behind many of my self-destructive tendencies in my early years. So, as far as my star status in the gym was concerned, my confused pubescent mind was made up: I would have to do everything within my power to avoid gaining weight.

My team trained after school for four hours a night, four or five nights a week with competitions and special training sessions most weekends. During that season, I was eating no more than 400-500 calories a day, and honestly, I don't know how I did it. After training, there was school homework to be done. Then, I would finally collapse into bed around midnight. Sleep was the precious prize that allowed me to forget everything for a few hours—a temporary escape from the misery of self-deprivation.

On Saturdays, if I was home, I sought relief from the week's intense pressures by binging on chocolate, sweets, and almost any food I could lay my hands on. But the indulgence was never worth the momentary pleasure. I allowed the numbers on the scale (which I kept beside my bed) to dictate my mood, emotions, and sense of worth. A day of binging always caused an immediate three to four-pound weight gain, so by Sunday morning, those numbers jeered at me with cruel vengeance and sent me into a downward spiral of despair. I would weep for hours under my blankets, devastated mentally by my own "failure." I was about eighty-five pounds at the time. If I went over ninety, I considered myself to be fat, worthless, and ugly. It was a relentless cycle of pain from which I longed to find freedom.

Like Mother, Like Daughter

Perhaps you're wondering where my parents were in all of this and why they didn't help me to overcome this eating disorder. To be honest, I don't really know. Like so many parents, it's possible they were so wrapped up in their own dysfunctions that they were unable to notice mine. My mother was struggling with an eating disorder of her own at the time. She would often go for days on a few lettuce leaves and a tomato, yet think nothing of tucking into a pound of nutritionally useless Callard & Bowser toffees while watching her favorite Saturday night TV shows.

My dad rarely commented on my lack of nutrition. Due to his long work hours, he probably wasn't even aware of it. Instead, he focused his disdain on my overindulgence of sweets and chocolates on the weekends that I was home. The intense shame I was encouraged to feel from eating these comfort foods contributed to my increasing inability to relate to food as a nutrition and energy source. It was a struggle that continued for nearly two more decades. Food was either my enemy or my emotional anesthetic; it was rarely anything in between.

Blessing in Disguise

At the age of fifteen, a severe injury forced me to retire from gymnastics. Sadly, this early retirement prevented me from competing for a place on the Olympic team. Looking back, however, I see my early departure from the sport as a blessing in disguise. The day I said goodbye to gymnastics, I felt an immense sense of relief. It was as though a heavy burden had been lifted from my young shoulders. Somehow along the way, I'd become trapped in a lifestyle that demanded everything I had and more. In truth, I don't really think I was cut out for the pressures that were involved. Early retirement opened the door for me to pursue a vocation in performing arts—something I'd been longing to do since I was eight years old.

Once I left the gymnasium, I began to eat more appropriately for my age and health. Nevertheless, all those months of malnutrition had taken a hefty toll on my body. During my final years of high school, I suffered with chronic fatigue syndrome, but despite it all, I launched headlong into a career of dance, choreography, teaching, and drama that started with five years of training at a top-notch performing arts college just outside of London.

Tug of War

I wish I could say my ordeal with self-image was over, but it had only just begun. Once again, I was on my feet from morning to night, and once again, a perfect physique and appearance were essential for success. Retiring from a sport that seemed to be killing me slowly may have been a welcome relief to my overtaxed body, but as far as physical output was concerned, I had jumped from a ruthless, weight-obsessed frying pan into an even hotter fire.

I was still disconnected from an understanding of my value, so it wasn't long before this internal confusion showed up again in another round of poor eating habits. In an effort to recover and replenish itself from all the years of nutritional deficiency, my body cried out for a sound and balanced diet, but the rebooted quest to be as thin as possible led to a tormenting psychological tug-of-war between overeating and crash dieting.

Smoking and Binging

A performing arts college wasn't a good place to be overweight. The teachers didn't mince words. It was drummed into our heads on a daily basis that a few extra puppy fat pounds could destroy our careers. The competition was fierce and the pressure was immense. I'll never forget the day the principal chewed us out for eating in between classes. She even threw a chair at my five-foot-nine-inch, 130-pound classmate for being "disgustingly fat, darling!" Samantha managed to dodge the chair, but the message came across loud and clear: eating was not only frowned upon and detrimental to our future, it was a serious safety hazard as well!

The stick thin teenage models in *Vogue* and *Harper's Bazaar* were my inspiration. Every inch of wall space in my bedroom was covered with glossy magazine images of the beauty I bowed down to. Eating almost nothing to remain model thin was a difficult task while dancing athletically all day long. Eating or not eating consumed my thoughts constantly. My classmates and I smoked cigarettes to take our minds off of the fact that we were starving. In my third year of college, I went through two packs of Marlboro a day, virtually chain-smoking in between classes—anything to put off the craving to eat a morsel of food.

The days I didn't eat much were the "good" days, but I frequently swung to the opposite side of the pendulum. On a "bad" day, I would eat five or six chocolate bars in one go, but never in front of other people; I did my binge eating in secret behind closed doors. There was much shame attached to the consummation of these comfort foods. Debilitating self-hatred over the weight these compulsive binges caused me to gain drove me to seek solace in the arms of anyone who was willing to accept me in my "obese" condition. (And when I say obese, I mean 120 pounds instead of the desired 110.)

Secret Hope

In my final year of college, I knew I had to pull myself together and get the weight off; my income would depend on it. The only way I could handle the task at hand was to revert back to self-inflicted deprivation tactics to get the job over and done with as fast as I could. By restricting my diet to four apples a day and a packet of Rowntree's Fruit Gums, my mission was soon accomplished.

Four months later, I was svelte, thin, and ready for auditions, but once again, the lack of nutrition in my diet left its mark on my health. Despite it all, the bottom line in my confused little head was this: thin meant job security and thin meant attractiveness to men. Deep down in my heart, however, what I hoped for most was for someone to be interested in *me*, the person I was inside, not just my physical attributes or faultless performances on stage and off.

I longed to meet a man who would say, "Hey, sweet girl, you don't *have* to work so hard, and you don't have to be *so* thin. Sit down and rest, and I'll take good care of you. I love you for who you are. No performance required." This longing was no doubt birthed out of an innocent desire to experience a sense of unconditional acceptance that was missing during my childhood. But, for all my longing, such a man did not show up in my life at that time. In the meantime, my toxic patterns continued. I simply couldn't shake the idea that I had to be underweight to be considered attractive and drive myself to overworked exhaustion to be financially secure.

Core Beliefs

We all have our bags of dysfunctional tricks, and these were mine. The memories of my childhood through to my mid-twenties seem surreal as I recall them now. It's ridiculous to think that I mistreated myself in the ways that I did, but I was a prisoner to my own misguided thought patterns, desperately wanting out, yet not knowing how to escape.

Eating disorders are just one example of the thousands of symptoms that stem from an absence of true identity and worth. Until *that* problem finds a permanent solution, all manners of behavioral painkillers, relational Band-Aids, and emotional crutches will fail to provide the inner security our souls are designed to experience. Our dysfunctional issues all stem from the same root: separation from our completeness in God. This, in turn, spawns ignorance and insecurity regarding our worth, quintessence, purpose, and identity.

Our mission of restoration, then, is two-fold: First, to reconnect to the Tree of Life and the divine Source of all love and life, and second, to uncover the negative core beliefs that govern our lives and replace them with core beliefs that are anchored in our *true identity* and *value*. Until we do this, we won't experience the lasting peace we long for; we'll continually miss the mark and live below our potential.

Hand in Glove

As twisted and as painful as those first twenty-five years of my life were, they were punctuated by some extraordinary seasons of creativity and vocational success. It often takes a brush with soaring heights and plummeting lows for an artist to produce their best work and I'm grateful for the memorable artistry that I was able to produce during that time. The pain and pressure of those roller coaster years also drove me to a crucial and pivotal point in my life: the day I called on the name of the Savior and found salvation in his everlasting arms.

That day should have been the turning point for a life that had, thus far, been governed by fear and a lack of self-worth. But it wasn't. My core beliefs of "appease to please" and "perform for security" had rolled over into my adult relationships and career. Now, like a hand in a glove, they also slipped perfectly into my newfound relationship with God. Like so many other well-meaning Christians, I completely missed the restorative totality of Christ's redemption—the sacrifice offered to deliver me out of striving and into secure rest. Instead, I fell hook, line, and sinker, for the idea that God is an authority figure who desires to be appeased with faultless behavior. On a subconscious level, I saw God as a powerful man (albeit a divine one) who approved of me if I performed well but frowned on me if I didn't. The deception was subtle, but it was there.

Doormat

After my salvation experience in California, the direction of my life changed dramatically. A brief engagement, a hasty marriage, and the conception of my first child took me into a vastly different world from the one I'd known up until that time. I felt relieved that the pressure to be stick thin had lightened a little, but it was quickly replaced with a new series of self-imposed pressures: to be a good and perfect Christian, a good and perfect wife, and a good and perfect mother.

Sermons that encouraged me to "go all out for God" and "make God proud" were right up my alley. I wanted to make my heavenly Father proud of me because I didn't want him to be angry with me. (This was a deep-rooted mind-set established in my childhood to offset my father's disapproving outbursts). As an actress and dancer, I was accustomed to pulling brilliant performances out of a hat. If that's what God wanted (and I thought he did), I felt sure I could deliver.

I played perfectly into the theology of servant-hood (though "doormat-hood" might have been a better term for me). My foggy sense of self-worth prevented me from differentiating wisely between laying down my life for Christ and allowing people to wipe their feet all over me. Sadly, some of the men I looked to for spiritual guidance gave me a hearty thumbs-up for my doormat mentality. In fact, some made good use of my confusion and gave themselves a good "shoeshine" at my expense.

Needless to say, during the formative years of my relationship with God, I lived far below the stature obtained for me by my Savior's ransoming sacrifice. My born-again birthday check representing "every spiritual blessing" (Ephesians 1:3, NIV) and "everything pertaining to life and godliness" (2 Peter 1:3, NASB) continued to sit un-cashed on the nightstand of my theology, and for many years, I missed out on the abundant life that had been purchased for me to enjoy.

Filter

Having dragged my poor self-image and fragile identity into my relationship with God, it was no huge surprise that I did the same thing in my marriage also. In the environment I was in, surrounded by headstrong, religious people, my lack of connection to my own voice and personhood translated seamlessly into the lifestyle of a mindlessly submissive pastor's wife.

I quickly learned that my former independence and professional success as a woman held little value in my new environment. This attitude, tinged with misogyny, played out in several of the churches we attended also. Women were acknowledged as being useful if they did a good job in the kitchen and served men to their liking. Like all good actresses, I internalized my new role and played it with commitment (just as my childhood vow subconsciously demanded of me), but it wasn't long before confusion set in and I couldn't figure out where cultural and religious obligations ended and I began. Entirely caught up in misguided religiosity, I failed to stand up for myself over some crucial personal issues. As a result, I tolerated degrading coercion for many years, all the while encouraged to believe it equated with taking up my cross and denying myself (Matthew 16:24, NIV).

I made the mistake of interpreting God's will for my life through the imperfect filter of my self-depreciating core beliefs as well as the self-centered conduct of the one through whom I experienced the coercion. These fear-filled, insecure thought patterns had been rooted in my subconscious since my earliest days. They were the warped and twisted lenses through which I saw my life and my relationships, including my relationship with God. Everything I needed for my own personal liberty was right in front of me, but I was too blind to see it. I couldn't see that I was both *permitted* and *empowered* to live in my redeemed freedom. The millstone of my childhood vows continued to hang heavy around my neck, imprisoning me in a lonely, harassed silence.

I did not know at the time that two more painful decades would pass before I escaped the unhealthy situation I was in. Just as in my growing up years, I was afraid to use my voice to stand up for the well-being of my own soul. I was afraid to take a stand for my own value and protection. I kept waiting and hoping for change or for rescue, but it never came. Once again, I believed that if I rocked the boat, I'd end up walking the plank. It was a lose-lose situation on every level.

Paradigm Shift

Saying "I do" will never be a recipe for wholeness and fulfillment. Anyone entering into marriage with the misunderstanding that it can fix what's broken in their own soul will receive their rude awakening sooner or later. Two broken halves cannot make a healthy whole. People cannot fix or save each other. A healthy union is only possible when two people take personal responsibility to connect with and draw from their divine Source.

Whether we're married, single, old, or young, if we're not

connected to the eternal and all-powerful Spirit as our Source, we will find ourselves seeking for a sense of value and identity in medicinal messiahs and substitute saviors. These counterfeits come in many forms: relationships, control, material possessions, work, career, power, success, fame, popularity, alcohol, food, pornography, romance, drugs, recklessness, sensual comforts, sexual encounters, and more. Though some of the things on this list are, of course, to be stewarded wisely for our pleasure, purpose, and productivity, they cannot ultimately provide the security and worth we're designed to experience. We need to establish a paradigm shift in our thinking; we must intentionally resist the temptation to medicate our pain and insecurity with things that aren't designed to satisfy our needs.

Religion tells us we need to "stop sinning" and to give up our medicinal messiahs because they're bad for us. And of course, many substitute saviors are severely detrimental to our souls; others keep us disconnected or distracted from our divine Source. But too often, religious teachings leave out the most important step to living a "sin free life." In giving up a go-to vice, something substantial must be provided to take its place, otherwise, the hungry void in our hearts will soon return. Our sense of "homelessness" will drive us back to our familiar "safe houses" and fixes—even if those fixes are unhealthy. The most important step in becoming free from dependency on substitute saviors is the integration and internalization of the truth concerning our origin, substance, and identity (discussed earlier in this chapter). We need to become "filled up" and established in the truth of where we came from and what we're made of. We need to know who we are so that we can be clear about what we're not. We need to recognize the abundance of all we have so that we can gladly turn away from the things that fail to satisfy. To know our value and arise in our fullest potential, we need an ongoing revelation of redemption, the gift that keeps us eternally connected to our home, our Source, and our completion in God.

Redeemed

The word *redemption* (in the Hebrew language) means, "ransom in full." This word is also linked with the ideas of separation and departure, reversal and completion. Biblical redemption, therefore, is a complete reversal of the separation and departure of mankind from his original connection to the source of life. It's our paid-in-full, one-way, express return ticket home to completeness and oneness with ourselves and with God.

As we learned earlier in this chapter, mankind was tricked by the father of lies and became blinded to the perfection of his own identity. He lost his awareness of the godlike similitude he already had. Mankind bit into the mindset of lack; he swallowed the lie that says, "What I need is missing. Who I am and what I have is not enough." In choosing to disregard the counsel of the supreme Spirit from which he was derived, mankind ate the fruit of the Tree of the Knowledge of Good and Evil. In doing so, he handed over his birthright of freedom and surrendered to the futility of religious striving. But, through Christ's obedience, the disobedience of the first man and woman was nullified. Through the sacrificial, atoning death of Jesus, all the effects of the fall were reversed. The ransom price for redemption was paid in full. We are now reconnected to God for all eternity. Every negative action that took place in the Garden of Eden was canceled out. "In him we have redemption" (Ephesians 1:7, NASB).

The complex word "redemption" in the Hebrew language also indicates that this complete reversal of separation and departure is linked to time, place, and relationship. That means right now, wherever we are and forever more, we can be one hundred percent connected to the life Source from which we're derived. We can rest securely in our true home—the eternal, omnipotent Spirit of God. We can flourish in partnership with the divine energy Source—the very power that upholds the universe.

Our worth is not something we can earn or achieve. Our identity is not derived from the quality of our performance or from the things we do. Our value is not dependent on people or things outside of ourselves. Our derivation and origin is God himself. We are made of "God stuff." Our priceless value is eternally established. Our incalculable worth is an unchangeable fact. We can be secure in our identity as the offspring of God. Arising in our potential is just a belief away—a belief that we're valuable because of what we're made of and where we come from. Belief is the connection cable to a never-ending Source of value, identity, acceptance, and love. As we believe it, we'll experience it!

Restored

Before I understood the cunning schemes of "the thief" and the magnitude of redemption, I felt like a puppet on a string pulled this way and that by ever-changing circumstances and emotional highs and lows. I saw life as a happenchance game of Chutes and Ladders (or Snakes and Ladders, as it's called in the UK) where my sense of security rose and fell depending on the quality of my day-to-day experiences. But circumstances, events, and relationships are *not* the dice that determine our rise and tumble on the game board of life.

The all-important game changer is restoration. The Hebrew word for restoration is *shuwb* (pronounced shoob), which means "to turn back, retrieve, reverse, set again." God's gift of restoration sets us back where we belong on the "winner's square"—the same winner's square that was ours in Eden, now purchased for us to enjoy through Christ's redeeming sacrifice. We are restored back to that top spot simply by believing it's ours for the receiving. Once we're there, we never have to vacate it. We can rejoice in the assurance that it *is* possible to maintain a steadfast connection to the Source of love and life even in the midst of fluctuating circumstances.

We can't re-run the clock and redo our lives. We can't go back to the Garden of Eden to prevent Adam and Eve from making the grave mistake that they made. But the great news is, we don't need to. Restoration (in Hebrew) also means, "to turn back without necessarily returning to the starting point." That means right here and right now, we can choose to declare it's a new day. We can allow redemption to take us home again. We can arise to a here-and-now Eden—a place of perfect peace and provision in God. We can choose to lay aside our shame, our fears, and every one of the negative perspectives we've dragged into our present from the past. We can choose to relate to ourselves, to God, to people, and to circumstances out of restored security and unshakable identity. Once again, we can live, move, and have our being in the surety of oneness and completeness in God. We can know without doubt that we're adequate, approved, accepted, and enough.

The incredible gifts of God's redemption and restoration are continually available to us. They are like a refreshing pool of water on a hot summer day, and our only appropriate response is to dive in and enjoy them! It's time for us to realign our beliefs with the reality of who we are, where we come from, and what we're made of. It's time for us to recognize and acknowledge our incalculable value and divine worth. It's time for us to arise in confidence to the royal stature to which we've been called.

It is time to arise.

It is time to know your value.

Reflections

_____

_____

_____

_____

_____

_____   _____

_____   _____

_____

_____

_____

_____

_____

_____

_____

4
Walk In Your Freedom

Trans-Atlantic Adventure

My first trans-Atlantic adventure to the land of the free and the home of the brave was at the age of thirteen with my gymnastics team. Our destination was Detroit, Michigan, where a well-planned itinerary of competitions, training camps, and exciting cross-cultural experiences awaited us. I will never forget the deliciousness of my first American pizza, and my first hot fudge sundae drenched in caramel sauce. In all my growing up years, I'd never tasted anything so good! In addition to these all-American culinary delights, having fun with our host families, dancing at the disco, and water skiing on Lake Michigan amidst the splendor of the Mid-West made this a teenage trip to remember.

Our overseas excursion also presented my team and I with an introduction to real outdoor heat—something we Brits rarely experience. On the outbound flight, when the plane refueled at Washington DC, we were permitted to stand on the exit staircase. I remember feeling as though I'd stepped into a giant planetary sauna. Never before had I experienced such intense humidity.

Another aspect of the United States that was fascinating to my young English eyes was the carefree beauty of the American girls. With their wavy locks and golden tans, they seemed to radiate a liberty of being I'd not witnessed in colder European climates. These images of freedom ministered deeply to my soul and certainly whetted my appetite for more. I loved the spaciousness of the big, blue skies and the cheery, warm sunshine. I enjoyed the positivity of the people and their generous smiles. When we boarded the plane for our homebound flight, I felt sure that one day I would return.

A Whiter Shade of Pale

Growing up in England where sunshine is a rare and treasured commodity, the chances of getting a golden tan are slim. At the mere hint of blue sky and warmth, Brits are typically found sprawled out on whatever deck chair or piece of emerald-green grass they can park their rear ends on. There you will see us, pant legs and sleeves rolled up with our faces turned toward the sun, exposing as much of our bare flesh to the rare radiation as is decently permissible in public. It is our silent, yet unified, national mission to make every ray of sunshine count.

When it comes to getting a beautiful tan, however, British melanin seems bent on maintaining a frustrating lack of response to sunlight. Instead of turning golden brown, our skin tends to resemble the sickly hue of an undernourished flamingo or a lump of uncooked salmon. With skin cancer on the rise, perhaps the fair isle-dwellers are better off. Whichever way you look at it, most citizens of the UK are stuck with their ashen skin. Unless they can swing a three-week "vaca" in sunny Club Tropicana, they're doomed to spend their entire year sporting a whiter shade of pale. It's possible my own English melanin has adapted to new climates over the years, or perhaps I've just had the good fortune to be blessed with a random, hereditary tanning gene. Either way, when I subject myself to sufficient sunshine, I can bronze to an enviable caramel color. I say *subject myself* because in Texas (where I currently live), the summers are blazing hot with temperatures hitting over 90 degrees Fahrenheit for weeks on end. Sunbathing in Texas, therefore, is less of a therapeutic pastime and more of a masochistic commitment to image. Though it's embarrassing to admit it, there *was* a short season in my life when I was wholeheartedly committed to that wannabe bronzed image. In fact, I still have the skin damage to prove it.

Flashback

Sunscreen is a must in the blistering American heat, but it seems that no matter how many times it's reapplied, it's only a matter of seconds before one's body is dripping with oily sweat from head to toe. One particular sizzling hot day, while stretched out on a sun lounger gasping for air, I noticed myself counting down the minutes until it was time to turn over. I was a steamy mess of perspiration and tanning oil and not enjoying myself at all. It was then I was struck with an alarming flashback of a recent shopping trip to Sam's Club.

The confrontation was uncomfortably disturbing. There the creatures were in my mind's eye, "sweating" with oil, turning over slowly and methodically until every square inch of their bodies was golden brown. The process was all too familiar. As if seeing their glistening limbs and torsos in a new light, I shuddered to realize how the roasting of poultry so closely resembled my own sunbathing rituals. There was no denying it. I had become like one of them. I had become like a Sam's Club rotisserie chicken.

From that day forward, it was difficult to take my tanning efforts seriously. I now find it hilarious to think of turning myself over from one side to the other to bake like a greased-up farm fowl until "cooked" evenly to glowing perfection. I *do* look better with a tan and don't miss an opportunity to bronze up whenever possible, but the mental image of those rotisserie chickens certainly keeps me grounded.

Mission

Venturing beyond rotisserie chickens and taking a closer look at the human race, it's not difficult to see that self-deceptive activity can be commonplace in many areas of our lives. My willingness to risk skin damage for the sake of temporary glamour is just one small example.

My mission heralded from a warped motive based on the deception that a tan, in some small way, could add to my value as a woman. As long as I remained convinced of that, it was likely I'd subject myself to whatever it took to accomplish my tanning goals, even if it was a ghastly, sweat-mongering process. It took a confrontation with roasting poultry to set me free from my masochistic, time-consuming pursuits.

The same root issues connected to self-deception or self-destructive behavior can apply to all manners of self-imposed "imprisonment." There's the ambitious workaholic, the perfectionist performer, the obsessive self-help fanatic, the overly competitive student, the control freak, the workout maniac, the suspicious spouse, the paranoid parent, and more. Of course, there's nothing wrong with working hard, doing our best, and going after success—it's important that we come into being as the best version of ourselves we can be. But if our overly excessive efforts are actually compulsive obsessive behaviors in disguise, then we have good reason for concern. If we find ourselves perpetually chained to the tyranny of the urgent, functioning like workhorses, convinced that "reaching the top" will solve all our problems, it's possible our motives are off kilter and in need of reevaluation.

Motives

In comparison to more life-threatening practices, my former, short-lived sunbathing obsession was of no great significance. But being bound by fear to *any* activity that's neither enjoyable nor healthy warrants internal investigation. "Michele, *why* are you doing this?" I asked myself. "Is getting fried alive *really* how you want to spend your time? Will the results *really* produce the lasting benefits you hope to achieve from them?"

Of course, I knew a tan could never make me the prettiest, the sexiest, or the most beautiful of them all, yet a tiny part of my heart was enslaved to the perception that it might at least contribute. My motive: to be physically attractive. The application: to do whatever it took regardless of the harm it caused me. The root: insecurity over my appearance. This slavery to self-destructive behavior stemmed back to the hidden core belief that so many of us form during early childhood—the belief that we are not enough.

Illusions

On the road to freedom, it's imperative we investigate our actions *and* our motives. Our motives can sometimes be self-deceptive. When our internal motives are off balance, our goals will be also. When our goals are off balance, we're in danger of becoming sidetracked from our destiny. Our motives, therefore, need to be screened thoroughly and often.

Fear and insecurity are powerful feelings. They can drive us to form goals based on illusions. They can lure us to devise dreams detached from reality. They have the power to bind us to the shady, ulterior motives within our hearts. In the process of chasing medicinal goals and dreams, we can become captives to our deluded causes and prisoners to our self-beguiling priorities. We're even capable of taking on an alter ego while traveling our rocky road to accomplishment. We want to walk in freedom, and we long for people to see the real us, but given room to dominate, fear and insecurity can cause us to become lost in translation through our own lack of internal clarity.

One Thing

King David was a master at streamlining his goals and bringing his focus back to worthwhile basics. He intentionally laid aside pursuits that offered only a *temporary* sense of freedom, significance, or security.

"One thing I ask from the Lord" he said, "that will I seek after: that I may dwell in the house of the Lord all the days of my life, to gaze on the beauty of the Lord and to inquire in his temple" (Psalm 27:4, ESV).

The same is true of Mary who set aside superfluous busyness in favor of listening to heaven-sent wisdom. Martha complained to Jesus about Mary's lack of get-up-and-go. She was frustrated that her sister was not pitching in to help her with her demanding to-do list. But Jesus commended Mary saying, "There is only one thing worth being concerned about. Mary has discovered it, and it will not be taken away from her" (Luke 10:42, NLT). It's worth mentioning at this juncture that being a "church meeting junkie" is not the same thing as sitting at the feet of Jesus. Even though we've promoted the phrase, "It's not about religion, it's about relationship," too many people fall prey to the bondage of a legalistic version of a relationship both with the church and with God.

All throughout my kids' younger years (when good babysitters were out of our budget), we packed up the diaper bags to attend congregational meetings every chance we could get. It was truly wonderful to hear the Word of God ministered so often, but the late nights and mealtime disruptions wreaked havoc on our family life and physical health. There's nothing wrong with being in church to get built up and edified, but with three small children to care for, it was neither appropriate nor healthy for us to be out every night of the week. We all looked like strung out Marthas instead of calm Marys. Clearly there was a codependent snag in our motives.

Acceptance

As parents called to ministry, I think we were afraid if we didn't show up to every meeting, our "lack" of attendance might be misconstrued as a lack of commitment to God or to the church. So even if it was inconvenient, we were in church every time the doors opened just to make sure no one thought the worst. Looking back, it's clear to me now: the motive behind some of that excessive attendance was fear of disapproval, not love for God.

It wasn't necessary for me to drag my children out to church every night to receive the wisdom and guidance God had for me, especially if the motive behind my efforts was rooted in fear and obligation. Our omniscient, omnipresent heavenly Father knows how to communicate with us in all manners of ways. He understands the seasons of life that we're in. He knows that raising three young children is an exhausting business and that getting sufficient rest to effectively build a godly home environment is equally, if not more, important than winning an award for Most Religious Meetings Attended. In everything we do, this fact remains: if our motives are toxic, peace will be lacking regardless of the apparent nobility of our actions.

It's imperative we realize that God has already given himself to us fully, unconditionally, one hundred percent, and forever. All that's required of us is to trust in the redemptive work of Christ, and live freely out of that assurance. "He has made us accepted in the beloved" (Ephesians 1:6, KJV). There is nothing more we can ever do that will add to God's total acceptance of us. Not even perfect obedience to God's Word can add to that acceptance. God's guidance benefits our lives, and following it opens the door to blessings and provision, but obedience cannot provoke God to love and accept us any more than he already does.

The Free Gift of Freedom

It's impossible for us to attain right standing with God by keeping religious laws, attending meetings, or volunteering until we're on the brink of exhaustion. "For it is by grace you have been saved, through faith—and this is not from yourselves, it is the gift of God" (Ephesians 2:8, NIV). We've been forever blessed with a Sabbath rest—a rest that allows us to cease from our own efforts as a means to attaining right standing with God. The search is over. The striving can cease. Righteousness has been given to us as a gift. The prison doors of our guilty conscience are unlocked forever and we are free. We don't have to "do time." We don't have to earn our way to heaven. It's through believing and receiving these absolute truths that we can walk in *genuine* freedom.

To each one of us, freedom will mean something slightly different at various stages of our lives. In our individual pursuit of freedom, however, we all share one common negative tendency: we put restraints on ourselves and allow fear and doubt to influence our beliefs. Too often, we live as though freedom is beyond our grasp. But the good news is this: the freedom intended for us to enjoy is already fully available. We were born into captivity to sin and death, but a "Get Out of Jail Free card" has been purchased for us through Jesus's atoning death, burial, and resurrection. When Jesus said, "It is finished," he meant it. The prison doors are open. All-inclusive freedom is ours.

Freedom is defined as "the power to determine action without restraint." It's the power of choice to think, speak, and do the right thing both for ourselves and for others. As we walk in freedom, we'll automatically demonstrate the joy of that liberty to others and our planet will be healthier as a result. Freedom is not just a state of being; it's a responsibility!

God's Mission Statement

There are millions of people in our world today who are enslaved against their will, physically confined, and completely unable to help themselves. My heart weeps for those who are subjected to abuse, exploitation, and atrocity. I can only be thankful the majority of us are not kept under lock and key suffering violent mistreatment and abuses too despicable to describe. Yet many still are, and they're in desperate need of rescue. May we do all we can in prayer and in action to help them.

The Son of God himself declared, "The Spirit of the Sovereign Lord is upon me, because the Lord has anointed me... to proclaim freedom for the captives and release from darkness for the prisoners" (Isaiah 61:1, NIV). "He has sent me... to set the oppressed free" (Luke 4:18, NIV). Without question, freedom, liberty, and abundant life are top of the list on God's mission statement for humanity. If we're bound, restricted, coerced, or uncomfortably obligated—if any aspect of our personhood is subjugated to involuntary servitude, then we're not walking in the freedom paid for us in full by our loving Savior. If our actions and decisions are born more out of guilt and shame than love and trust, it's time for us to take a closer look at our hearts, lives, and motives.

Transparent Gold

In the New Testament, gold represents our faith—refined, tested, and proven to be genuine. It also represents the purity and authenticity of our hearts. As the new covenant temple of the presence of God, it's helpful for us to observe how the first temple in Jerusalem was overlaid with genuine gold. The Old Testament book of First Kings describes the building of Solomon's Temple and the prioritized application of a solid gold overlay in the rooms within that consecrated house.

When the Temple was built, the first area to be overlaid with gold was the inner sanctuary, which represents the innermost places of our hearts. The second part of the temple to be overlaid with gold was the altar. The altar represents the motives upon which our actions and sacrifices are made. If we want our "inner sanctuary and altar" to be like pure, transparent gold, honesty will be essential. In the process of refining our innermost thoughts and motives, we need to be transparent with ourselves, with God, and with others. Self-deceit will prevent us from experiencing personal revival and genuine transformation. Only the truth sets us free.

Whether we realize it or not, our subconscious beliefs are the "command center" for our experiences. Therefore, regardless of whether our current truth is good or bad, it's crucial we uncover it so that we can get real about what's governing our thoughts, emotions, motives, and actions. It's possible that some of the beliefs we've come to rely on as truth might be leading us into bondage and captivity. To arise in truth that sets us free, we must first let our own truth arise. We need to uncover the crossed wires in our subconscious belief systems so that they can undergo replacement or repair. Only when our beliefs are consistently in alignment with God's words and universal principles will we begin to walk in the freedom we yearn for. Getting in touch with our own truth and our own inner voice is sometimes easier said than done, but it is a necessary step to walking in freedom.

Spill the Beans

One cold and bleak New Year's Day, around the time I was living in my "pit of despair," I decided to take a long walk to consider the morbid reality of the traumatizing situation I was in. I set out with one intention: to be uncompromisingly honest with God, and with myself, about absolutely everything. I determined I would hold nothing back. Whatever the truth was with regard to my thoughts, emotions, circumstances, and relationships, it was time to spill the beans, even if it was ugly.

As I started out along the quiet residential street, tree branches around me creaked and strained, bracing themselves against the numbing winter wind. Deep within the avenues of my soul, gates of repression strained in resistance also, but the crowbar of honesty was already at work prying the prison doors open. Tears etched their way down my cold, reddened cheeks. The icy wind blew hard against my face as if to further ridicule the oppressed condition of my heart. I wasn't but a few steps beyond my street corner when the torment of my pent-up pain began to surface. The ease with which my suppressed agony began to pour forth shocked me at first, but having given myself both permission and mandate to be ruthlessly honest, it was obvious the sealed caverns of my emotions were peeling open. Already I knew, there was no turning back.

Tell It Like It Is

Had I known such a torrent of sorrow would be unleashed from within me that day, I might have opted for a more tranquil holiday activity. Gut level honesty has a way of making things messy for a while. Being a neat freak at the time, I wasn't thrilled about the way this interlude of self-awareness was messing with my stoic English calm. I strongly considered throwing in the towel on my tell-it-like-it-is venture, but just as in the living of life, I was already halfway down the hill to Harmony Park and I'd already covered much ground. There seemed little point in turning back to the way things were.

As I walked, I talked out loud, into the air, to myself, to God, to the past, but most of all to the people who had hurt me and abused me. In my mind, I saw their faces. With the eyes of my heart, I looked into their eyes. I said what I meant, and I meant what I said. I cried, I wailed, I despised, and I was real about it. All the shoved down, bottled up, stuffed in, grievous expression of trauma I'd been experiencing (and hiding) for so long began to exit my soul with venomous vocabulary.

The knots of indignation that had been imprisoned in my muted heart unfurled with fire into the surrounding silence.

Had religious bystanders been close enough to witness my verbal distress, they might have been tempted to hurl a stone or two in my direction to put me back in my subjugated, religious place. But once again, I sensed Jesus's support as my champion Defender in an hour of great need. As I released my anguish and torment, my Savior upheld me and encouraged me. Like a kind and faithful companion comforting a drunken friend while they vomit foul-smelling puke into a nightclub toilet, my Beloved unflinchingly remained by my side. As the true friend he is, he waited out my expression of darkest despair in favor of helping me become whole.

It was as though the silent scream within my soul had finally found a voice. The real and honest truth of my feelings spewed forth until words became insufficient. Doubled over in convulsing sobs, barely able to catch my breath, one thing became absolutely and unquestionably certain: From that moment on, I couldn't and wouldn't permit myself to continue suffering in the same way. The buck would stop here. It *had* to.

Stuck

Having reached the bleachers at the end of the soccer field, I climbed to the top row and looked out over the field into the distance. I felt calmer now—exorcised. But to my surprise, it wasn't long before a new torrent of anger churned up within me. This time it was aimed at an unexpected target, and it caught me completely off guard.

Since the day we met, I'd never turned a blaming finger toward my Savior. Anger toward God, in my opinion, is nonsensical on every level. But whether I liked it or not, confusion and frustration were very present in my heart. Now that the floodgates to my innermost thoughts had broken open, strong emotions were surfacing forcefully, and they refused to be pushed back down.

Suddenly, I heard myself screaming at the skies. "Why did you let this happen to me? Why did you let me suffer all these years? Why haven't you protected me and rescued me?" Until that day, I was unaware how shaken my faith had become. I knew I'd been hurt and betrayed by men, but now I was discovering I felt abandoned by God as well. My feelings had been encapsulated in a prison of fear, but now at last, they were finding a voice.

True Feelings

Our true feelings aren't always easy to face, but we must allow them to surface if we're to process our pain with understanding and arise in genuine freedom. Sitting there, shivering in the chill of that solemn New Year's Day, I could see that I was stuck. The "same old, same old" was killing me slowly—eroding my weakening hope. It seemed that no matter how much I'd prayed and pleaded with God to rescue me from my traumatizing circumstances, nothing had changed for the better. The wheels of life were still turning efficiently enough to "Keep Calm and Carry On," but nothing altered the fact that my deeply troubling situation needed intervention and resolution.

The fact that so many years had passed and God still hadn't "opened the eyes of the blind" and come to my rescue led me to wonder if God actually cared about me. I was beginning to resign myself to the belief that this must be it—this must be my miserable lot in life: quiet suffering behind closed doors—a thousand extra miles with a painted-on smile to keep the ministry ship floating down the river. In my heart of hearts, I didn't believe I was experiencing God's best for me, yet in all this time, I hadn't seen evidence of his help or deliverance either. To many, my life appeared enviable and starlit, but deep down inside,

I felt horribly forsaken. It was actually a welcome relief to acknowledge how I truly felt, both to myself, and to God.

Good Things

Having bared my soul and poured out my heart, I needed some big answers to some big questions. Weary and undone, I sat down and waited. As time passed, the clouds thinned and the wind died down. A ray of golden sunshine broke through the bleak, gray skies onto the frozen landscape. Instinctively, I turned my tearstained face toward the light and took a long, deep breath. Then I took a dare: "Give me something to hope for, God," I whispered into the breeze. "I'm still willing to believe in you."

Warming words from heaven alighted upon my broken heart, and sooner than expected—words that changed the course of my life from that time on. Embracing them became the first step toward a new beginning. I heard the Spirit of God whisper, "Michele, I have good things for you, good things." This simple yet profound statement was everything I needed to shift my perspective; it was a foundational truth I could hold onto for the rest of my days.

My Savior assured me he had never left me or forsaken me, even in the severest of trials. He let me know he *had* seen everything I'd experienced, and he wasn't happy about it, not one bit. Silent suffering was *not* the plan he had for me. A traumatized existence was a far cry from the abundant life he'd paid for me to enjoy. My Beloved had good things for me, *good* things. Hope was resurrected in my heart that very hour.

Responsibility

The revelation that my life was intended to be filled with good things changed everything for me. It was as if I'd finally seen the light. Scales began falling off my eyes. I wasn't *meant* to accept junk in my life, and it was up to *me* to say, "No" to it. Poor treatment is junk. Oppression is junk. Abuse, of any kind, is junk. For the first time, it dawned on me: We have a God-given right to be free. We have a God-given right to say, "No" to mistreatment in our lives. We not only have a right, we have a responsibility!

I had unknowingly become angry with God because I thought it was *his* job to make the oppression go away. Not only that, but deep down in my subconscious belief system, I'd bought into the idea that in certain areas of my life I was required to just put up and shut up—that I mustn't rock the boat—that it was all just meant to be. I was stuck in a miry muck of misconceptions about the gospel. I needed to understand that taking up my cross didn't mean getting hit over the head with it. The bottom line was this: I wasn't walking in the freedom that was available to me, and it was high time I did.

During this time of reflection, Proverbs 23:7 (NASB) came to mind: "As he thinks within himself, so he is." There it was, the perfect description of my problem. In my heart, I didn't believe I was deserving of good things or good treatment, and I had allowed people to relate to me accordingly. My circumstances had become a reflection of my innermost thoughts and beliefs. I needed to make an adjustment in my thinking. I needed to replace my current, *perceived* truth with *real* truth. I needed to replace my negative thoughts toward myself with positive thoughts—thoughts that aligned with my true value.

Taking a Stand

Once I realized I was neither forsaken nor forgotten, I took a fresh step of faith toward the promises of God. I began to accept the idea that I *could* be the recipient of good things. I saw that it wasn't my job to be the catchall for someone else's selfishness, addictions, behavioral disorders, mood swings, or damaging codependency issues. I realized that if I wanted to experience love, it would have to start with me loving myself first, and caring for myself enough to step away from bondage, oppression, toxicity, and mistreatment. For the first time ever, I held up a metaphorical STOP sign to all the junk I had thus far tolerated. At last, my journey toward genuine personal freedom had begun.

The walk back home was an uphill climb. It was symbolic of the struggle I was about to encounter in taking a determined stand for myself. Fueled by new perspectives, I made the decision to fearlessly face every arduous challenge that lay ahead of me and dare to believe for good things every step of the way.

It wasn't easy to be so forthright with God or with myself that day, but doing so uncovered some erroneous core beliefs that I hadn't realized were governing my choices. Acknowledging this junky "truth" for what it was enabled me to reject it so that I could embrace God's *higher truth* for my life. It was honesty that made the way for this powerful shift.

One of the definitions for honesty in the dictionary is "freedom from deceit and fraud." I had been numbing down my pain and staying quiet about the things I was suffering behind closed doors. The motive for my silence was fear. I knew if I revealed what was happening, there would be a dramatic fallout that could affect many people. Nevertheless, the fruit of that fear was a form of self-deceit that kept my entire situation in stalemate. The willingness to be gut-wrenchingly honest changed everything. Instead of covering up my feelings, I courageously exposed them. I also sought out a trustworthy counselor with whom I could confidentially share the things I was experiencing. From then on, I was able to replace lies and misconceptions with dependable truth and walk in genuine freedom.

Slick Cover Image

I wonder how many people remain bound to strongholds in ugly circumstances because they're captive to self-disparaging beliefs they perceive to be truth. Here's the litmus test: If we're not activating our power to make healthy, happy choices, we're not walking in freedom. If this is the case, we need to have an honest talk with ourselves, with God, or with whomever we perceive is restricting our freewill. The best time to get honest about our "stuff" is often. There's little point in wearing a mask or stifling the truth. There's nothing we can do or say that will surprise God; the omniscient Spirit already knows everything about us and is familiar with all our ways (Psalm 139:3). Psalm 51:6 (NASB) says, "Behold, you desire truth in the innermost being" or "you desire integrity in the inner self" (HCSB).

Trying to maintain a slick cover image is one of the chief preventatives to walking in freedom. We have to ask ourselves what we *really* believe about our lives, our situations, our relationships, and about God. It's also important that we know what we want— not what we *think* we want, or what we think we *should* want, but what we *really* want. Once that truth has been brought to light, we can begin the process of letting go of any belief or desire that does not align with the *good* things intended for us to enjoy.

Burying our feelings keeps them locked up, then who we are as a person becomes locked up with them. Acknowledging our thoughts and feelings appropriately in an environment of safe counsel brings them into the light and exposes them for what they are. The shackles of fear and secrecy are broken. Wisdom has an opportunity to enter in, leading us to personal adjustment, healing communication, and a reconnection to redemption.

The Proof of the Pudding

Jesus promised us truth that sets us free: "If you remain faithful to my teachings... you will know the truth, and the truth will set you free" (John 8:32, NLT). "If the Son sets you free, you are truly free" (John 8:36, NLT). It's worth mentioning that many religions and inspirational teachings attest to offering this same freeing potential. In my own exploration of freedom, however, it is the Word of God, written and embodied in Christ, interpreted in the light of grace, which has proven to be the most liberating on a consistent basis. We have to be picky about what we ingest into our belief system. There's an old English saying that says, "The proof of the pudding is in the eating." In other words, the pudding might *look* delicious, but only tasting it will prove how delicious it really is. In the context of walking in freedom, the proof of the pudding is the way our lives look after we've been chewing on our beliefs for a while. If our theologies and thought patterns result in bondage, stress, and bad fruit, we're probably eating the wrong pudding and need to take a closer look at what we're biting into.

Pure and Simple

Real truth and godly beliefs are like good nutrition that nourishes us for the long haul. There are all kinds of foods for sale in our grocery stores, but only a closer inspection of the ingredients label will help us to distinguish between good nutrition and junk food. We can save ourselves a lot of unnecessary effort, however, by heading straight to the produce aisle, especially the organic section. I don't know about you, but if I attempt to sustain my body with foods containing a myriad of chemicals and genetically modified ingredients, I feel very out of sorts. But when my food intake is organic, my body feels strengthened, and I'm nourished to function at my optimum best. In the same way, to arise in our potential and genuinely walk in freedom, we must regularly inspect the ingredients of our lives and the spiritual food we're ingesting.

James 1:27 (NKJV) describes a quality of relationship with God that's pure and undefiled. When it comes to the gospel, the good news of God's eternal, unconditional love for mankind, we need to be wary of man-made additives and "genetically modified" twists. These additives can be toxic and detrimental to our spiritual health. The fruit of the Tree of the Knowledge of Good and Evil is exactly that—a demonically inspired, genetically modified, toxic counterfeit to the life-giving goodness of God.

One of my favorite Scriptures in the Bible talks about pure and simple devotion to God: "I am afraid that, as the serpent deceived Eve by his craftiness, your minds will be led astray from the simplicity and purity of devotion to Christ" (2 Corinthians 11:3, NASB).

The meaning of these key words is enlightening. Devotion means "earnest attachment to a thing or a person." Pure means "unmodified, free from foreign or inappropriate elements, and free from extraneous and contaminating matter." Simple means "easy to understand and deal with, not elaborate or artificial, unaffected and uncomplicated." Our relationship with God needs to be this way: pure, simple, devoted, and organic—one hundred percent free from man-made fillers and additives. If our devotion to God is pure and simple, an uncomplicated and authentic relationship with God will result.

Comfort Zone

I was in South Africa when I first discovered the beauty of pure and simple devotion to Love. Although the circumstances of my life were hugely overwhelming, the deepening relationship I developed with the Holy Spirit during that season was beautiful, real, and uniquely personal.

My cookie hadn't crumbled the way I expected. So much had happened within a short space of time. Whether I liked it or not, I was stranded in a strange place with strange people, completely out of my comfort zone. The events that led up to my second continental move in less than nine months seem bizarre as I look back on them now. Admittedly, with an older and wiser head on my shoulders, they're not something I would care to repeat.

It had been a year since I'd boarded that January flight to Los Angeles in search of solutions for my heartache and emptiness. My intention had been to spend four months in the United States and then return to my teaching position in London. But that plan was drastically altered two days into the trip when I asked Jesus to be my Savior and Lord—a decision that turned my whole world right side up. Two weeks later, I met a fellow believer at a church group for single adults. We quickly became Bible reading and prayer buddies.

Fast-forward four months and I followed what I thought was God's direction for my life by giving up my return ticket home to London. It was a bold step indeed; I didn't have a work visa for the United States so I couldn't get a job. I knew it wouldn't be long before I would run out of money and then food. Though it's likely I mistook foolishness for faith, in my youthful zeal, I felt sure I was doing the right thing. Without knowing the details of my (self-inflicted) plight, like an angel, Francis showed up at my digs with several bags of groceries. Encouraged by the evidence that God was aware of my situation, I continued to hearken for my next set of instructions.

Warning Signals

A little less than five months after we met, the man from the Bible study suggested we get married, and for some elusive reason, I agreed to the idea. The fact that neither of us felt any "in-love" feelings toward each other should have been a huge warning sign that we were not doing the right thing. No doubt there were numerous subconscious, codependent motives in operation that neither of us had the self-awareness to recognize at the time. My fiancé's father kindly helped me to obtain an extension to my visitor visa and to organize a flight out of the US back to the UK. But my final flight destination was Johannesburg, South Africa, the birthplace and homeland of my husband-to-be.

It's difficult to imagine what my parents must have thought about these sudden, new developments in my life. If they were concerned, they didn't show it. I had been earning a living and taking care of myself since I was sixteen and was grateful for the trust my parents placed in me. So, with their apparent agreement, completely unaware of the years of emotional and psychological anguish that lay ahead of me, off I went to Africa. I thought I'd experienced culture shock in Los Angeles, but soon discovered that the west coast of America was child's play compared to Johannesburg. At the time of my arrival, the whole nation was in a state of political, economical, and cultural unrest. As a launching ground for two people who barely knew each other entering the challenging realms of marriage and parenthood, South Africa couldn't have been a worse pick.

Upheaval

The marriage ceremony was held in a little Assemblies of God church in Hillbrow, Johannesburg. During that decade, Hillbrow was known to be one of the most violent cities in the world. The wedding was a sad and lonely affair for me; there was no one in attendance that I knew—not one person. Six weeks after I said, "I do," I was pregnant with my first child.

Through two continental upheavals, I had said goodbye to my job, my friends, my family, and my country. Everything familiar to me was now gone. I wanted the chance to go back in time—to rethink my choices and make wiser decisions, but it was too late. The marriage felt strained from the start. Issues that I hadn't been aware of during the engagement period came to light immediately after the wedding. Months of unemployment added to the stress of that unsettled season. Our living conditions were cramped and resources were scarce; there was little comfort to be found in anything.

I needed to find my Redeemer again in a real and uncomplicated way. All the man-made fanfare and clutter would have to be set aside. Emotionalism portrayed as passion for God would have to be ditched. I desperately needed a genuine encounter with the Savior to help me face the overwhelming challenges that lay before me.

Overwhelmed

There's nothing more powerful than the Word of God. Psalm 138:2 declares that God's name and Word are exalted above all things. Yet in my stressed and fragile condition, trying to absorb even a few verses a day as a "baby believer" seemed more than I could handle.

True to character, my gentle, compassionate Savior was never bent out of shape over my temporary disposition, not even for a second. (Jesus, I've discovered, isn't religious at all.) He understood that the complexities of his Word were too much for me to take in at that time. He had no intention of overwhelming me with more than I could handle. He was aware of the pressure I was experiencing on every level of my life and did not want to add to it. He was not concerned with how many Bible verses I was reading each day—which version, what time, or how often. God had a plan to extend his love and comfort toward me in simpler ways. He too desires a relationship with us that is pure and uncomplicated, free from man-made additives and the clutter of religious obligations.

He chose to wrap his arms around me through the illustrated pages of a children's book—*Alice in Bibleland* to be precise. Early in the morning, when no one else was around, I would pull out Alice's guide to The Lord's Prayer. In the colorful pictures, cute little Alice had blonde pigtails and wore a pretty blue dress; she looked to be about eight years old. Feeling as unsafe as I did, I could relate to her frail vulnerability and childlike desire for protection.

Safe

One page of the book meant more to me than any other. Alongside the phrase "Our Father" of The Lord's Prayer, Alice's commentary was: "God you're like a parent, you teach us and you guide us, and like a loving parent, you're always there beside us." And there was Alice in the picture—snuggled up in her mummy's lap, embraced in loving arms—safe, protected, and at peace.

For months and months, I internalized the message conveyed through that touching imagery. It represented everything I most needed to know during that frightening season: God is my protector; in his arms, I am safe. These droplets of manageable truth were fed to me by God's own gentle hand the way a shepherd might feed a lost, orphaned lamb. Through this tender mercy, I received the comfort and strength that I needed in a palatable and uncomplicated way. My only appropriate response was pure and simple devotion—the very reflection of God's heart toward me. Years later, as my mother lay motionless in a coma, suspended between life and death, I knew how to reach her. I understood the power of simplicity and its profound contribution to freedom.

Cancer

I knew my mother had been diagnosed with colon cancer, but I was unaware of the degree to which her physical condition had deteriorated. In our overseas phone calls, she and my dad would always avoid the subject of her health. "We don't want to worry you, dear," was their benign mantra. The British National Health Service was a slow-moving machine. My mother's name had taken months to surface to the top of the surgery list. The appointment to remove the cancerous tumor in her bowel was finally scheduled, but she weighed only seventy pounds upon admittance to the hospital.

I was living in Danville, Virginia at the time of her surgery. We weren't well off by any means. My [former] husband was managing a bookstore and studying for his bachelor's degree in theology, and I was mother and home educator to our three rambunctious, young boys. Trying to make visits to England was challenging both financially and logistically. My mother didn't enjoy travel due to a lifelong battle with Meniere's disease, and her ever-worsening colon cancer prevented her from enjoying the primetime years of her life in the way she deserved. On the day of her hospitalization, I was daunted by the realization that several years had passed since I'd seen either of my parents.

Turbulence

When the call came to let me know that my mother had suffered a stroke and multiple organ failure as a result of her surgery, we scrambled for a plan to get me to England as soon as possible. Two days later, I was on a plane to London not knowing if my mother would still be alive when I arrived. The long flight was emotionally agonizing. The plane encountered some of the worst turbulence I've experienced in all my years of flying—an outward manifestation, perhaps, of my inner turmoil and distress.

I'd become familiar with the ominous message of the Bible Belt South that warned if you didn't come to church, walk the aisle to the altar, repeat the sinner's prayer, and publicly profess Jesus as your Savior, you wouldn't make it into heaven. This contrived list of requirements for salvation echoed torturously in my thoughts for the entire twelve-hour passage.

My mother hadn't walked down the aisle of a church since her wedding over forty years earlier. Discussing faith with her was disdained, yet I'd never heard her verbally reject the idea that Jesus was who he said he was. Fortunately, and thanks to the movie *Jesus of Nazareth* starring Robert Powell, she was familiar with the plan of salvation. When I was a child, we watched the film on television together almost every Easter. She always appeared to be moved by the story, but never verbalized her feelings and thoughts about it.

After living and preaching in several American states, I'd become privy to a broad spectrum of denominational practices and perspectives extraneous to the Word of God. On that long flight across the Atlantic, I wrestled with religion. I had to sort out the basics again. It was time to rightly discern real from fake and hold fast to the truth that could set my mother free—nothing artificial added.

The idea that my mother might not meet the requirements for heaven based on the harsh judgments of an angry preacher didn't seem right. Instinctively, I knew it wasn't.

Holding On

From plane to tube to train to taxi, I tumbled, trembling, into my mother's hospital ward. "She's still holding on," the nurse encouraged. "Come this way." Nothing could have prepared me for what I saw next. I approached her bedside slowly, trying to take it all in. Her frail body lay frighteningly still under a thin, white blanket. The image before me was beyond comprehension. She was ashen and skeletal and only a few strands of hair lay across her otherwise bald scalp. My formerly beautiful mother resembled an aging corpse removed from its coffin and cruelly laid out on a gurney to haunt me. Aside from shallow breaths aided by machines, she appeared lifeless. Though only sixty-eight years of age, my mother was virtually unrecognizable as the woman I once knew. It was unbearable to see her this way.

The nurse removed the breathing mask from her face so that we could "converse" more humanely. (The throat and nose tubes were left in place.) I couldn't tell if she was able to hear me or if she was aware that I was even there. Still governed by the mindset that some kind of prayer would be required by my mother to be acceptable in heaven's heart, I whispered a prayer within my own. "God, if there's something my mum needs to do so that she can be with you in heaven, please, somehow, let her know. Give me the right words to say. God, please, have mercy on my precious mother!"

Simple Words

My mind raced. There was no guarantee how many hours or minutes she had left to live. There was no time for semantics or theology. An explanation of the plan of salvation was too much for her to take in. There was no way she'd be able to say "the sinner's prayer." An altar call would be of no effect here. I had to believe that the God of the universe desired to welcome her into paradise, and that he would willingly receive her if her heart so much as flickered a desire for the same.

One simple sentence came to mind that said everything I could hope to say, yet it required only a simple, silent nod of affirmation within my mother's heart to secure her safe passage home. I leaned close to her ear. "Let Jesus hold you, Mum," I said. "Let Jesus hold you." Suddenly I knew; if the message in those simple words wasn't enough for a soul to be saved, nothing was. In the end, that's all any of us can do really isn't it: acknowledge our inability to save ourselves and surrender to the trust that there's a Savior who desires to hold us close as we pass from this world to the next?

I repeated those same words over and over. I *willed* her to hear them. Suddenly, from her motionless coma, as she hung with unspeakable vulnerability between earth and eternity, my lovely, sweet mum turned her face toward me. As though blinded by a dense fog, yet somehow aware of my presence, her eyes opened slowly and searched for mine. She moved her mouth to speak yet remained inaudible. One huge, solitary tear rolled out of her tender blue eye all the way down her right cheek. Then, slowly, her eyes closed for what was to be the final time here on earth. Somehow, I knew she'd heard me and that everything was going to be okay.

Departure

My father, brother, and I agreed with the doctors to put my mother on a life support machine to see if she could pull out of the coma and make some kind of recovery. In retrospect, it was a huge mistake and only prolonged the inevitable; we all regretted the choice. After a week, it was determined that she wasn't physically capable of making a recovery. Once the decision was made, she departed almost immediately.

After the funeral, I became tormented with fear, suddenly unsure if my mother was in heaven. One night, about three weeks after returning to America, I broke down and wept, desperate to know clearly one way or another. I cried out to heaven, begging for closure: "God, please tell me! Where is she now? Where in eternity is my beautiful, sweet mum?"

My plea for resolution was answered within a few short hours. In a clear and vivid dream, I saw my mother lying on what appeared to be a hospital bed covered in white. I remember thinking to myself in the dream, "Why is my mum here? Why is she back in the hospital?" I walked closer and realized that she wasn't in a hospital at all, nor was she wearing a hospital gown. She was wearing a pure white celestial robe! I saw her look up at me and smile brightly. She looked more radiant and beautiful than I'd ever seen her before. "Mum, you're alright!" I exclaimed. She sat up energetically and wrapped her arms around me. "Yes, I'm alright!" she said, with great joy. "God has done this!" Immediately, I woke up and sat bolt upright in bed. The room was filled with the glorious, tangible presence of God. All anxiety and fear left me. I knew beyond a shadow of a doubt that my mother was in heaven, and I've never doubted it since.

Amazing Grace

Telling the story of my mum's final hours is always deeply moving for me. It's not just because she's my mother, or because it was tragic to lose her so early. I become stirred at the remembrance of her twilight moments because they're the sweetest melody of grace I've ever known—grace, that up until that time, I hadn't fully understood.

The precious time I spent with my mother in the last hours of her life not only affected her eternity, but it also became the catalyst for a deep transformation within my own heart. In her dying breath, as she whispered her frightened plea to a Savior she barely knew, he saw the merest reach of her heart toward him and regarded it as great faith. Without hesitation, and moved with compassion, the champion Defender came swiftly to her rescue. Wrapping her up in his tender mercies, he carried her to safety in the realms of his love. No doubt an escort of angels was in attendance, their gossamer wings cooling her sickly brow. There she lay, draped over the Savior's redeeming arms, his frail princess, Sylvia June. He placed her on a bed of Sabbath rest and angels dressed her in white. Giggling together at the thought of my untold delight, they planned for her to sit up and surprise me in my dream. "I'm alright!" she rehearsed with joyous freedom. "God has done this!" Then three weeks later, I heard those incredible words for myself and knew she was saved forever by God's kindness and grace.

My beautiful mother's sunset on earth became my liberty, my dawn, and my arising. I cannot help but tell everyone I meet: "The Lord is compassionate and gracious, slow to anger, abounding in love... he does not treat us as our sins deserve or repay us according to our iniquities... he remembers we are dust" (Psalm 103:8, 10, 14, NIV). "His understanding, no one can fathom" (Isaiah 40:28, NIV).

The night I saw my mother in heaven, God proved to me he is not a hard taskmaster. He doesn't crack a whip over our backs expecting us to do much with little. In his grace and mercy, we can breathe, trust, and find rest from the unbearable burden of the law. *Only* in this grace and mercy can we walk in genuine freedom.

Let Freedom Ring

Defining freedom is one thing, but walking in freedom for a lifetime requires brave decisions and determined steps in a specific direction.

> *It is for freedom Christ has set us free. Stand firm, then, and do not let yourselves be burdened again by a yoke of slavery... The only thing that counts is faith expressing itself through love. You were running a good race. Who cut in on you to keep you from obeying the truth? That kind of persuasion does not come from him who calls*

you... You, my brothers and sisters, were called to be
free."

Galatians 5:1, 6–8, 13, NIV —

These powerful verses contain a statement, a warning, and a question. The statement is this: It is for freedom that Christ set us free. This freedom is not a partial freedom or a compromised liberty. It's a full and complete freedom to be embraced wholeheartedly and stewarded wisely. And thus we're warned; having received freedom, we're not to become entangled in a yoke of slavery.

Knowing this, the all-important question we must ask is who or what keeps us from our freedom? Have we prostituted our souls to the binds of relational and circumstantial slavery? Has a yoke of oppression been forced upon us from which we must find courageous escape? Have we become the instigators of our own restrictions, limiting ourselves through imprisoning beliefs? Have we buckled to peer pressure or yielded to comparison and no longer feel empowered and at peace?

Whatever forms our bondage may take, we must press in to identify the source, the root, and the nature of our chains. As we're honest about our innermost thoughts and feelings, we'll be able to identify the deceptive motives and negative core beliefs that keep us bound, and replace them with reliable truth. We'll be empowered to disentangle our souls from oppressive forces and toxic attachments, and wholeheartedly walk in the freedom made available to us.

Second Corinthians 3:17 (ESV) says, "Where the Spirit of the Lord is, there is freedom." As we invite God's liberating presence into our hearts and minds, and embrace pure and simple devotion to love, we'll be free to live authentically as our noblest and truest selves.

It is time to arise.

It is time to walk in your freedom.

Reflections

_____

_____

_____

_____

_____

_____

_____   _____

_____   _____

_____

_____

_____

_____

_____

_____

_____

5
Live In Your Vitality

Vital Force

Vitality. What a brilliant word! Just the sound of it makes me feel like juicing something or going for a jog. Vitality is defined in the dictionary as "the capacity for survival" and "the continuation of a purposeful existence." Vitality also means "exuberant strength or mental vigor" and "the power to live and grow." Perhaps best of all, vitality literally means "life force."

Like me, you've probably lived through a good many ups and downs in your lifetime. No doubt you've accumulated a large collection of "been there, done that T-shirts" to prove it. You know what it feels like to live in survival mode—to go through the motions, hoping to scrape up enough energy simply to get out of bed. You also know what it feels like to be on top of your game—operating in your gifts and talents—connected to the things that make your life feel worthwhile.

In our world, negative forces are at work seeking to steal our vitality, annihilate our aspirations, and derail us from our purposes. I'm thankful to say, I've never experienced the physical violation of burglary or theft, but I do know what it's like to have my hopes invaded and my dreams broken into. There are many things out there that can drag us down or throw a wet blanket over our zeal for life, but the same God who gave us freedom is calling us to arise in an even greater experience of liberty—vitality!

Vitality is the unlimited power of divinity within us, activated by faith, expressed in purpose, and experienced through connection to our identity and uniqueness. It's the motivating force that empowers us to persevere through difficulties and withstand everything that tries to break us down. Vitality is the dynamite fuel that ignites our inner fire and makes us feel truly alive!

Romeo and Juliet

My first brush with this kind of vitality was at the Covent Garden Opera House in London when I was eight years old. I was with my parents to see The Royal Ballet performing *Romeo and Juliet* to the Prokofiev score. The featured lead dancers were none other than the illustrious megastars of the ballet world, Dame Margot Fonteyn and Rudolf Nureyev. The atmosphere in the auditorium was electric. As I waited with innocent anticipation for the curtain to rise, I had no idea that the general direction for more than a third of my life would become established by the end of the performance. The staggering chemistry between the prima ballerina and her "forbidden" beau was intoxicating to me. I sat, awestruck, on the edge of my seat as passion, tenderness, grief, and love were conveyed through exquisite movement and stirring music. What I saw, heard, and experienced that night moved me to tears and profoundly shook my world. Though I was too young to assimilate the details of such a passionate relationship between a man and a woman, in the depths of my soul, I understood it.

Freedom of Expression

Though no words were spoken during the performance, I was introduced to the life-changing power of dynamic and effective communication. That night, for the first time, I became aware of the relationship between my own unique personhood and the role I was to play on the planet. I recognized that artistic expression was to become a key player in the tangible outworking of my God-breathed life force.

During my professional career, I didn't have the opportunity to perform on a stage as formidable as that of the Covent Garden Opera House, but I did have the privilege of working as a choreographer, dancer, actress, and director in many venues in and around London's

West End theater district. It was wonderful and engaging work. Teaching and choreographing at the Italia Conti Academy of Theater Arts in London offered me an even deeper level of artistic satisfaction for it was in *this* work that I was granted the greatest freedom of personal expression.

Over the years, my résumé expanded beyond acting and choreography to include motivational speaking, poetry, theater arts direction, writing, teaching, coaching, play writing, and more. There have been many times over the past few decades when I've felt unsure of my artistic identity, but my calling finally made sense when I realized I'm not limited to any one creative genre. Though the forms of expression might vary, the foundation and essence of my lifework remain the same: the communication of stories, messages, and ideas for the purpose of enrichment, encouragement, awakening, and growth.

Caged

Vitality can seem illusive. We might need to seek hard to identify what it is that makes us feel fully alive. For many people, a connection to vitality shows up in something specific. For others, discovering what makes them tick can be a complex journey. Getting to the place where *who we are* lines up with *what we do* is a process. For some, it's a longer process than for others, but when our personal design is activated and cultivated, we flourish like a rose bush in springtime. One area of vitality seems to trigger another and then another. At times like these, we better understand the words of Jesus, "I have food to eat of which you do not know" (John 4:32, NKJV). There's nothing more satisfying than being fed and sustained by one's own inner vitality and purpose!

Conversely, the same gifts that fuel our focus can become a source of internal frustration if they're caged or hindered. Closed doors, unemployment, or unhealthy micromanagement are just a few of the challenges we might face in the pursuit of living in our vitality. Just because we happen upon our purpose doesn't mean everyone around us will be supportive of our mission.

Our natural gifts can get buried or shelved, and the same can happen with our *spiritual* gifts also. Within each one of us, there's a "safety deposit box" filled with all kinds of natural and spiritual treasure. Too often, however, we live with this treasure locked away. Too often, the bounty within us remains untapped and unseen by those who would benefit greatly from all that we have to share.

Tenacity

Regarding their vocation and function, many people make the mistake of waiting to be discovered—sitting on their gifts until someone gives them permission to shine. In doing so, they may wait an entire frustrated lifetime for their vitality to be released. Living in our vitality requires us to open the lid to the treasury of who we are. The ingredients for a life of vitality are deposited within us, and we, ourselves, possess the combination to the safe. We hold in our hand the keys to the lock, but it's up to us to use them. Finding the right place to operate in our vitality might take a determined search, but we've been promised: "Ask, and it will be given to you; seek, and you will find; knock, and it will be opened to you. For everyone who asks receives, and he who seeks finds, and to him who knocks it will be opened" (Matthew 7:7–8, NASB).

Several years ago, a young music artist approached me asking if I knew of a performing arts high school in his area. I was aware of several in London and New York—schools where students are tutored in their academic work *and* developed in their artistic gifts all under one roof—but these schools aren't common in the southern states. I told the young man that I knew of no such school, but encouraged him to keep working hard and to make the most of the opportunities before him. He followed my advice, but remained undaunted, calling me every week throughout the spring and summer to ask the same question. He was thoroughly convinced the answer he'd heard wasn't the final one.

Then, to my surprise (but not his), I received an email from an address I didn't recognize informing me of a brand new high school for the performing arts opening in the fall. Auditions were being held the following week. When I saw that the school would be located five minutes from the singer's house, I realized it was an incredible answer to prayer. He auditioned successfully, received the artistic and academic training he was hoping for, and went on to become successful in his field.

This aspiring artist's story is a wonderful example of how passion, faith, and tenacity can work wonders. He was determined to knock on doors until the right ones opened so he could get where he needed to go. Even when circumstances appeared unfavorable, he didn't give up, but echoed the words of King David in Psalm 27:3 (NIV), "I am still confident of this: I will see the goodness of the Lord in the land of the living." The young man loved himself enough not to give up on his gifts and dreams. He continued to believe in his own personal destiny even when he ran into opposition. He recognized that loving himself in this way was a vital component to arising in the fullness of his potential.

Shot in the Arm

Scripture instructs us to "'Love the Lord your God with all your heart and with all your soul and with all your strength and with all your mind' and to 'Love your neighbor as yourself'" (Luke 10:27, NIV). Loving God and loving others makes sense to most of us, but loving *ourselves* is the part we seem to struggle with the most. Loving ourselves is something God really wants us to get a grip on. It's a crucial element to living in vitality because it opens us up to the all-important awareness and appreciation of our own unique design and potential.

Loving ourselves also includes self-nurture, listening with compassion to the voice of our own souls, and making room for our own needs to be met. By treating ourselves with kindness and respect, we teach others how we want them to treat us. Most people will not love us any better than we love ourselves.

As we travel along life's winding road, it's important we give ourselves a regular shot in the arm concerning who we are and why we're here. In the New Testament book of Philemon, Paul says, "I pray that the sharing of your faith may become effective by the acknowledging of every good thing which is in you in Christ Jesus" (Philemon 1:6, KJV). Many people are afraid to acknowledge the good things that are in them; they're concerned they might become proud or arrogant if they do. But this acknowledgment is nothing more than the vital recognition of the awesome things accomplished in us and restored to us through redemption. As we boldly acknowledge the gifts that reside within us, we are able to activate them both for our own benefit *and* for the betterment of the world around us.

The good things in us are the foundation of our vitality. They are ours to exercise, develop, and use for positive influence. It's essential we know what these good things are so that we can draw from them and use them productively and effectively. This understanding will not puff us up; instead, it will create within us a humble confidence that is not easily shaken. In the wise words of Gilbert Chesterton, "It is always the secure who are humble."

Dark Shroud

To live in our vitality, it's essential that we cast off its antagonist: false humility. False humility is the depreciation of our own divine likeness, talents, gifts, and assignments. Too many potential world changers wear this religious shroud believing they're doing God a service. But thinking poorly of ourselves prevents the kingdom of light and love from being established through us. Jesus instructed us: "let your light shine before others" (Matthew 5:16, ESV). Paul advises us beautifully in Romans 12:3 (GWT) "not to think of yourselves more highly than you should. Instead... use good judgment based on what God has given each of you as believers." In other words, we shouldn't try to operate in strengths we don't possess, but we shouldn't hold back on using the gifts we've been given either.

We've been given exciting work to do and all the tools we need to accomplish it, but failing to acknowledge our strengths keeps our sharpest and most powerful tools locked away and unavailable for use. Acknowledging our weaknesses is important for healthy growth, but allowing our weaknesses to *define* us is a slap in the face to God. False humility cripples us into a mindset of inadequacy and defeat. It causes us to undervalue our strengths and become absorbed with our weaknesses.

Psalm 139:14 declares: We are "fearfully and wonderfully made." Galatians 2:20 (NLT) says, "It is no longer I who live, but Christ lives in *me*." (Italics mine.) God is excited and confident about the *"me"* he lives in. He wants us to be excited and confident about ourselves too! He's chosen to express himself through the gifts, talents, and personality traits he's placed within us. When we hide those treasures, we rob the Creator of opportunities to touch others' lives through our own.

Que Sera, Sera

The story of John the Baptist provides us with a wonderful example of a man who was willing to lay aside false humility to embrace his purpose and live in his vitality. It's important to note that when John was questioned about his identity, he declared who he *wasn't* before declaring who he *was* (John 1:19–23). Defining our specific calling sometimes requires us to go through a detailed elimination process of who we're not so that we can determine with clarity who we actually are. Nothing dulls our vitality more than trying to be something we're not. We tire easily when we're not operating in the strength of our own unique design. Not only that, but desiring to walk in someone else's shoes can give rise to jealousy, envy, backstabbing—even betrayal. Negative emotions such as these can quickly lead us away from our purpose and prevent us from embracing our own significance and mission.

A little mentioned fact about John is his heritage in the priesthood of Israel. At the time of John's conception, his father, Zechariah, was high priest. (Zechariah was the man to whom the Angel of the Lord had appeared with the news that he and his wife, Elizabeth, would bear a son even in their advanced age—Luke, chapters one and two.) I'm sure Zechariah had big plans for his "surprise" son to continue in the traditions of the priesthood. If anyone had their life mapped out ahead of them, John did, but "Que Sera, Sera" was not to be his theme song. Instead of high priest, God had called John to be a prophet with an unusual and extraordinary message. This required him to break away from the traditions of his fathers. No doubt John encountered many raised eyebrows and critical comments as he courageously followed the call on his life, yet he devoted himself fully to the task he was given. Unmoved and undaunted by the pressures and expectations of the people around him, John followed his heart and became God's powerful, prophetic voice to Israel—the voice that prepared the way for the Savior of all mankind. John connected with his internal treasure, shunned his naysaying critics, and fulfilled his destiny. His example of obedience continues to serve as an inspiration to us all.

Seasons and Transitions

Ecclesiastes 3:1 (ASV) says, "For everything there is a season, and a time for every purpose under heaven." Living in vitality means connecting to the specific purpose that is ordained for us in each season of our lives. Like John the Baptist, there will be times when we're in a different season than the people around us. During such times, we'll need to display tenacity and determination in order to stay anchored to our purpose and focused on our assignment. We might also need to exercise a willingness to embrace unexpected tasks as they come our way. John's assignments included that of outspoken prophet *and* obscure prisoner. He was called to two alarmingly different roles within a short space of time, yet both required his focus, agreement, and obedience.

The very nature of vitality includes growth. Growth leads to development and development leads to change. As we move from one season to another, our purpose or occupation might change and our focus might need adjustment. Strategies and perspectives that worked for us during previous assignments might need to be laid aside and replaced with new strategies more appropriate for the tasks at hand. What worked for one project may not work for another.

Resisting change can create frustration and lead to confusion. It can also cause us to make poor decisions at a time when we need to exercise courage, flexibility, or patience. Whatever leg of the journey we're on, we need to accurately assess each unique season's purpose. It's possible to experience peace and productivity in every season of life, but we must be willing to embrace each opportunity for what it is and glean good things from every moment we're given.

Transitions from one season to another provide us with an excellent opportunity to reevaluate what ignites our vitality. Transitions also give us a chance to fill up our "spiritual gas tanks" and receive a "heavenly oil change"—the fresh anointing needed for a new project or focus. If something in our soul is damaged, transition times provide us with an opportunity to pull over to the side of life's fast moving highway and fix what's broken. We can make the most of transitions by embracing new perspectives and letting go of what no longer serves us. In doing so, we will enter each new season of purpose well equipped for all that lies ahead.

Scattered Treasure, Broken Jewels

Living consistently in our vitality while navigating our way through life's twists and turns is a challenging business. Traumatic, challenging, and heart-wrenching experiences have a way of clouding our vision and muddying the path of our direction and purpose. Painful trials have a way of dulling the unique radiance that exudes from our hearts. Our gifts and talents can become stifled or scattered, leaving us doubting our adequacy and questioning our abilities. Fatigue can swallow up exuberance. Our "go-getter" energy can fade to weariness. Simply put, hard times can cause us to lose touch with the beauty and brilliance of who we are.

Many years ago, I attended a prophetic presbytery hosted by a reputable church in North Texas. As I was being prayed for, the pastor saw a specific image in his mind's eye. The picture was that of a large treasure chest—the kind that might have been carried on a sixteenth-century sailing ship. In the vision, the pastor saw himself approach the chest and open the heavy, ornate lid. When he peered inside, he saw that the treasure was *me*. The concept that I am "treasure" became a significant factor in my inner healing process. The simple imagery helped me to see myself in a new way—beautiful, ornate, valuable, and precious.

Several years later, during an especially traumatic season near the closure of my marriage, I was moved to tears during a time of prayer. Suddenly, I became aware of my Savior's gentle presence in the room. I closed my eyes and sat very still to hear what he might say to me. Unexpectedly, in my mind's eye, I saw a small, unfurnished room. In the center of the room, there was a treasure chest with an open lid. Intuitively I knew, it was the same treasure chest described to me years earlier by the pastor at the presbytery. As the "vision" continued, I saw the figure of a man enter the room. He leaned over the chest and began rummaging aggressively through the contents. His movements were harsh and forceful; it appeared from his actions that he was looking for something specific. He glanced briefly at each of the jewels, but when he saw that none of them satisfied what he was looking for, he carelessly strew them aside. Eventually, in frustration, the man gave up his search and walked away, leaving the damaged treasure all over the ground.

Tender Care

I wept as I looked at all the broken jewels. I realized the man and his actions represented a lifetime of disregard shown for my feelings, my freewill, and my personhood. It was a painful image to process. Tears began falling down my cheeks as I embraced the reality that for many years I had experienced little, if any, nurture or cherishing warmth in my personal relationships.

Then something very beautiful took place. Jesus stepped into the picture. He slowly walked around the chest and bent down to pick up all the precious jewels from the dirty ground. I could see that he was deeply saddened by the indifference shown toward the valuable treasure—treasure he considered as being his very own. Piece by piece, he held the fragments in his hands. With his robe, he gave each one a gentle and adoring polish before carefully laying it down inside the chest.

As I watched the scene, I was aware that God himself had crafted each jewel with his own hands, and by his loving touch, each one was restored. His sincere and tender care for each piece of treasure was symbolic of his care for each part of *me*. The sense of his concern for my safety and well-being was unmistakable. To be cherished in this way brought great consolation and solace to my heart.

When all the pieces had been gathered from the floor, repaired, restored, and placed back in the chest, Jesus gently closed the lid. He didn't close the lid to conceal me or to confine me. He closed the lid to show me that I was in control of the boundaries in my life. No longer should I permit people to dig around selfishly in the treasure chest of my heart. No longer should I allow people to exploit me, use me, or show disregard for my feelings and well-being.

The fact that such deep restoration was necessary felt grieving, but seeing the vision presented me with an opportunity to reevaluate the treasure that I am. It also helped me to see that I needed to choose carefully where and with whom that treasure might be invested. It gave me a chance to reassess who I am in God's eyes, and to take a new inventory of my greatness and value.

During my marriage, I had allowed many gifts and treasures within me to become dormant and inactive. I'd also shelved many hopes and dreams and allowed prophetic promises that were personal and important to me to become buried and forgotten. How beautiful it is that Jesus doesn't forget or forsake any of these unique things about us? He demonstrates his concern for every single part of us and ensures that nothing is forfeited or lost. Regardless of how we've been treated in the past, we must always believe in the value of our personhood and nurture ourselves with tender care. Our vitality depends on it!

Enjoying Me

Jesus's compassion also helped me to realize our greatest calling is simply to *be* treasure—unique and precious—cut, carat, and design. We're amazing in God's sight, adored and dearly beloved. This delight God has for us is something we need to feel for ourselves also. The phrase "enjoy yourself" is typically used in conjunction with participating in activities, but I like to think of enjoying myself from a different perspective; I want to learn to enjoy *myself*—to enjoy everything about who I am.

Enjoying ourselves is dependent on knowing and *accepting* ourselves, and appreciating the individual qualities of our own unique being. We flourish in vitality when we honor ourselves for the masterpiece that we are. Recognizing our own treasure helps us readily recognize the treasure in others also. Our relationships take on new value and our interactions come alive when we value the intricate distinctions of each person we engage with. In an environment of recognition, acceptance, and appreciation, people are set free to enjoy themselves in ways they may never have thought possible, and to thrive in the beauty of their own unique personhood.

Purpose

If vitality is the "aliveness" that surges through our veins, purpose is the heartbeat that initiates it. Discovering, pursuing, and living a purpose-filled life is essential to experiencing vitality. Bahamian Bible teacher and author, Myles Munroe, said, "When the purpose of a thing is not known, abuse is inevitable." This profound statement applies to almost everything! Potential remains dormant and untapped when purpose and function are not understood.

Purpose is "the reason for which something exists or is made." If we don't understand our purpose, we will struggle to maximize our potential, and our vitality won't be activated to its fullest extent. Many people go through life disconnected from their purpose and design, floundering, sometimes for years, to determine the best direction for their life. But finding the right path can be less complicated than we make it out to be. We're on the right road to purpose and vitality when we do the things we're gifted to do—the things we love and enjoy. Our purpose is connected to the vitality we feel when we engage in the causes and endeavors we feel passionate about.

Discovering Purpose

Clarifying our life purposes may require some sincere soul searching. Therefore, to successfully navigate our voyages of discovery, it can help to ask some probing questions: What gives me joy? What do I love doing? What am I good at? What activities tend to make me lose track of time? Who and what inspires me and why? When I've reached the end of my life, what do I think will have mattered most? What would I hate to regret? If I had a message to communicate to the whole world, what would it be? How can I use my gifts and talents to make a difference in the causes I feel passionate about?

As we answer these, and similar, questions, it's helpful to identify the key *action words* that show up most often in our responses. For example, I find myself using the verbs "communicate, encourage, empower, and awaken" when I ask myself the above questions. These action words resonate with my gifts and desires; they clue me in to my passions and purpose. We also need to identify our goals and aspirations by asking questions such as: "Who are the people I most want to serve, help, reach, entertain, etc." And, "how can I benefit these people while doing the things I most love to do?" By combining our key action words with our goals, we'll be able to craft a personal mission statement that essentially represents our purpose and our strengths.

A personal mission statement empowers us to make wise and intentional choices. It helps us to filter out the "unnecessary weights" from our lives—the extras that clutter our time and give us double vision. These nonessentials hinder us from arising in our greatest potential and hold us back from walking energetically in the direction of our destiny. Not everything that shows up on our doorstep should be invited in; not everything that comes our way belongs in our lives. Distractions that steal our strength or blur our vision need to be laid aside.

Answering probing questions to uncover our passions and purpose might seem difficult at first; the process of discovering the authentic greatness of who we are can be challenging. But one essential ingredient in the journey that we cannot do without is a willingness to let go of what we think we *should do* and who we think we *should be* based on social pressures or cultural norms. We arise in vitality by confidently embracing our authentic selves. We come into being by allowing the *true* colors of our unique treasure to shine with radiant clarity and brightness.

Razzle Dazzle

At the risk of casting a cloud over our sparkle, it's worth remembering that "shine" might not always be equated with glamour. In the real world, our day-to-day purpose might end up being anything but glitzy. Years ago, as a young mother of three boys all under the age of five, my average day included running errands, cleaning up vomit, participating in toy gun stakeouts, calming teething babies in the middle of the night, conjuring up nutritious meals on a shoestring budget, preparing lesson plans, and conquering insurmountable piles of laundry. If I managed to get in the shower by 4:00 p.m., I considered the day to be a raving success.

As a gifted artist, there were occasions during those child raising years when I wondered if the lack of artistic creativity in my day-to-day life would snuff out my inner light. But even then, there was always a sense of purposeful exhilaration in my heart gracing me to go the long haul with excellence. Raising my three amazing men was a far cry from a "razzle-dazzle" lifestyle, but daily, I was cognizant of the eternal investment being made. As I look at my sons' lives today, there is no question that being their devoted mother and home educator will always be the most important thing I've ever done or ever will do.

Open Hand

Parenting should always be considered a long-haul venture, but I've discovered, there are *some* endeavors for which going the long haul is neither sensible nor beneficial. We need to be mindful that success or failure within a certain field should not prevent us from taking on something new from time to time. Most people take on several different purposes in their life span. Provided our motive is not escapism, it's healthy for us to embrace fresh possibilities, especially if the things that once vitalized us no longer do.

Paying close attention to our "internal vitality gauge" helps us align with our purposes and callings in each new season. A diminishing sense of vitality can be a warning signal that indicates change or adjustment is needed. We must be careful to neither allow fears about the future or nostalgia over the past to lead us away from new assignments and divine promptings. Unwillingness to relinquish the familiar can hold us back from the next stage of our destiny. We need to be willing to "open our hand" in surrender—to allow the removal of things which no longer belong. When we do this, our load is lightened and space is made for us to take unhindered strides on unchartered pathways. In transitions, we're often given only one small step of guidance at a time, but as we faithfully walk in the light that we have, we'll successfully find our way to new shores of purpose.

Mandate

Over the years, I've had many opportunities to put my internal vitality gauge to good use. Making a decision about my kids' education was certainly one of them. I remember debating with myself over and over whether I had what it took to be a successful homeschooling parent. Did I have the patience, the grace, and the ability? Would it be a blessing or a nightmare? I pondered the dilemma for nearly two years.

At the midnight hour, with the Pre-K registration deadline for my oldest child just three days away, God spoke to me through Hebrews 11:7 (NASB): "By faith Noah, being warned by God about things not yet seen, in reverence prepared an ark for the salvation of his household."

At the hearing of this prophetic guidance, peace settled into my heart and vitality was ignited in my body and soul. I understood from this verse that I was to prepare an "ark"—a safe place for my kids to learn and grow away from extraneous pressures and the systems of this world. Aside from devoting time to core academic subjects, I was excited for the extra hours my boys would have to develop their individual creative talents (especially since all three of them were artistically inclined).

It's worth mentioning that despite having received a divine directive to homeschool my children, I felt no more equipped after God's words came to me than I did before. I possessed a heartfelt passion for the assignment, but it continued to feel like a precarious endeavor for many years. Grace for a long-haul appointment is rarely dumped on us at the starting line of our journeys. Instead, it is given to us day-by-day as we walk out our responsibilities in obedience and (blind) faith.

One of the greatest challenges I faced in making plans to homeschool my children was the sense of inadequacy I felt for the magnitude of the task that lay before me. I had opportunities to learn from other home educators in my community, yet despite my deficiency of experience, I knew I wasn't to compare myself to them. Having been called to homeschool my kids, I had to trust that I would be anointed for the mission. I was, after all, the one most acquainted with my children's hearts and learning styles. I knew the only way to effectively tackle the test before me was to equip myself the best I could and "walk by faith, not by sight" (2 Corinthians 5:7, ESV). Though I often felt the ogre of fear breathing down my neck during those challenging years, I discovered that the vitality experienced in following a God-given mandate trumps every circumstantial giant.

Do What Works

When it comes to claiming victories over circumstantial giants, David is a shining example. As David prepared to fight the giant Goliath, King Saul offered his own defensive armor for David to use. But the brave teenager graciously declined. Though young in age, David recognized that Saul's armor had been specifically designed for Saul; it didn't fit right on David's body and would have been more of a hindrance to him than a help. David's weapon of choice was a simple slingshot and stones. This option probably appeared ridiculous to onlookers, but it was a weapon David had become skilled in using. He stuck with it because he knew it would work for *him* in the situation he was in. The result: he slew Goliath quickly and efficiently and won a mighty victory for his people.

David declined the use of Saul's defensive armor in favor of an offensive weapon—a weapon he could handle with confidence.

Choosing an offensive action that we can handle with confidence is a great strategy for overcoming all manners of challenges in our lives. It was David's shameless ownership of his own unique qualities combined with his relentless zeal for the task at hand that empowered him for victory. We can't fight our battles in a way that works for someone else; we have to do what works for us. There'll be many times in our lives when we'll feel overwhelmed by circumstantial giants or pressured to solve a problem someone else's way. But if we passionately apply our gifts and creativity to the tasks before us, like David, we also will be empowered for victory.

Fire in My Bones

Throughout all fifteen years of my homeschooling journey, I weathered some pretty hefty personal storms. Yet on almost every challenging day, my heaven-sent calling to educate my children burned like fire in my bones. It was a fire that kept my internal light shining brightly even when darkness was pressing in hard.

The term "fire in my bones" was used by Jeremiah regarding the prophetic messages he was asked to speak to the people of Israel: "His word was in my heart like a burning fire shut up in my bones; I was weary of holding it back, and I could not" (Jeremiah 20:9, NKJV). Jeremiah certainly didn't enjoy *every* aspect of his assignment from God; in fact, much of it was fraught with suffering and pain. But compromising his calling drained him of his strength and vitality. Just like this courageous prophet of old, we don't relish every moment of our calling either, but the vitality we experience along the way holds us to our course.

Without Measure

Spiritual fire is not just available to an elite few; it's available to everyone. It's the power of the Holy Spirit—the *same* power that raised Jesus from the dead. When we invite the Holy Spirit into our hearts and lives, a mighty force comes to live within us. It's as though we become plugged in to the universal energy Source of all love, life, and power.

The Holy Spirit is described as the Spirit without measure—an unlimited, inexhaustible resource of everything we need for any task at any given moment. The Bible declares that God "is able to do exceeding abundantly beyond all that we ask or think, according to the power that works within us" (Ephesians 3:20, NAS). It's important for us to notice the "within us" part of this verse. These words indicate that the power of God is manifest and released in and through *people.*

God promises: "If the Spirit of him who raised Jesus from the dead dwells in you, he... will also give life to your mortal bodies" (Romans 8:11, ESV). To arise in our fullest potential and live in our vitality, it's essential we allow the dynamic power of the Holy Spirit to take up residence in our lives. Ephesians 1:23 (ESV) says we are "his body, the fullness of him who fills all in all." As vessels of the almighty Spirit, we fill the earth with God's power and presence. No wonder God wants us to be confident about the good things that are in us. Not only do we have a message of redemption and reconciliation that positively transforms lives, we have the power to confirm that message, "not in persuasive words of wisdom, but in demonstration of the Spirit and of power, so that your faith would not rest on the wisdom of men, but on the power of God" (1 Corinthians 2:4–5, NASB).

Activation

Experiencing the vitalizing life force of God shouldn't be confused with getting out of bed on the right side or consuming the best combination of caffeinated coffees and herbal supplements. The power to arise and live in our vitality is activated through the simple belief that we're connected to an almighty power Source, and that "whatever you ask for in prayer, believe that you have received it, and it will be yours" (Mark 11:24, NIV). Spiritual power is activated through our intentional alignment with the power Source within us and through divinely inspired acts of faith.

I experienced this "activation through faith" in a very practical way in Argentina some years ago. I had flown in to speak at a miracle service being held in the capital city of Buenos Aires. Advertising for the service had been widespread. There was a great sense of expectation among the host leaders. On the night of the event, the venue was full to overflowing. Many of the people in the crowd had serious physical needs. Some were blind, deaf, or terminally ill. Many were struggling with depression, generational iniquity, or situations of domestic violence. This wasn't a good week for the speaker to be sick, but as timing would have it, I was.

I can only imagine there must have been mold in the walls of my aging hotel room. As sensitive as I am to environmental allergens, I felt the effects of the irritant quickly and severely. By the second day of the trip, I was struggling with respiratory issues. My bronchial tubes were inflamed, and my throat was closing up. A few hours prior to the miracle service, I still had a small, scratchy voice, but unbeknownst to the event leaders, by the time we got to the third worship song, I had full-on laryngitis. I tried to speak but not a sound could be heard.

I sat in my chair mouthing the words to the songs, but inside, I was panicking. I'd been praying over this event for weeks. I knew I had an important message to deliver. I also knew I was carrying an anointing to pray for healing miracles. We were about to see great and mighty things! The problem was, I had completely lost my voice. "What shall I do?" I asked God frantically in my heart. "Show me how to handle this!" I felt a reminder deep within my spirit that the same power that raised Christ from the dead was able to quicken and revitalize my body. "Carry on as planned and trust me," I heard the Lord say. I tested my vocal chords out a time or two more during the final worship song, but there was no change. Fully aware of God's mighty power residing within me, I made up my mind to follow the instructions I'd been given.

Miracles

I stepped up to the platform and something amazing happened. From the moment the microphone was placed in my hands, my voice could be heard loud and clear! For forty-five minutes, I delivered God's message of hope to the people. Then for the next two hours, the ministry team and I prayed for hundreds of people to be healed from debilitating physical ailments. Miracles took place and many of the people were healed. It was an extraordinary night. Until the very last "amen" my voice was clear and strong. Once the ministry was finished, however, my vocal chords closed up again, and my voice did not return to its normal strength until over a month later. I learned by experience that night: the power of the Holy Spirit is manifest both in us and through us as we activate our faith and partner with God in his loving purposes.

Spiritual Vitality

Spiritual vitality is experienced through the awareness and activation of the good things that are in us. Through this awareness and activation, we can arise in a vitality that holds firm regardless of circumstances. As we tap into this power on a daily basis, we can become conduits of mighty blessings on the earth.

It's easy to recognize people who've tapped into their internal vitality. It's as though they carry their own sunshine regardless of the weather. When they walk into a room, the atmosphere changes for the better. They possess a contagious confidence and magnetism. They're fueled and ignited by a limitless life force that emanates from within them—a force that cultivates life wherever they go.

Beyond exciting relationships, meaningful occupations, and all manners of stimulating circumstances, the eternal life force of God within us is our truest and most reliable source of vitality. When we activate this vitality, we experience a supernatural "of him, through him, to him" lifestyle (Romans 11:36, KJV) that sustains us, enriches others, and brings honor and glory to God. This lifestyle is a partnership with creative Source energy for which we've been fully equipped and empowered.

Unity

Before he was crucified, Jesus prayed to the Father saying: "I have given them the glory that you gave me, that they may be one as we are one—I in them and you in me—so that they may be brought to complete unity" (John 17:22–23, NIV). The word *glory* in the original Greek of this text means "dignity and honor." This verse of scripture is telling us that Jesus gave us the same glory—the same dignity and honor the Father had given to him.

Though it might seem extreme of God to bestow his glory upon us, we shouldn't be surprised at his generous gift. Jesus chose to impart to us his own dignity and honor for the purpose of bringing us into effective partnership with him. As an illustration, consider the president of the United States. The president works in collaboration with a vice president whom he or she appoints. If the appointed second-in-command were not given appropriate honor and recognition as the president's dignitary and right-hand person, an effective partnership between the two would not be possible. In fact, that man or woman wouldn't even make it past White House ground security, let alone into the Oval Office.

In the same way, God "raised us up with him and seated us with him" (Ephesians 2:6, ESV) and "blessed us with every spiritual blessing" (Ephesians 1:3, NASB). God brought us into "complete unity" (John 17:23) with himself and gave us dignity and honor as his co-laborers as well as "boldness and confident access through his faithfulness" (Ephesians 3:12, ISV). We're positioned, appointed, empowered, and anointed for effective and influential partnership with God.

Intimate Connection

The Messiah was mindful of God's original intention for man when he chose to bestow his glory upon us. In chapter three (Know Your Value), we studied the origin and essence of mankind and learned that we're made in God's likeness—born of the eternal, omnipotent life force—similar, comparable, and of the same spiritual substance. We learned that man's *awareness* of this similitude was lost when he swallowed the lie that he needed to become more like God (though he already *was* like God). We grasped that mankind's intimate connection with God (through likeness) was broken when man assimilated the poison of doubt into his being regarding his glory and comparable personhood. We learned that connection to our divine Source is reestablished and activated when we receive, and continue to receive, the fullness of Christ's redemption gift—the gift that restores to us all that was lost in the Garden of Eden.

God's intention has *always* been unity and oneness. He accomplishes this oneness by making two "parties" comparable and of the same substance and likeness—God and man, Adam and Eve, and now Jesus (the last Adam) and his bride. It is for this reason Jesus called for *his* glory to become ours in John chapter seventeen. In making this request, Jesus was preparing us for the redemption that was about to be accomplished through his death on the cross. It was as though he was mantling us with our bridal covering, making us ready for intimate unity through the fellowship of restored likeness.

Moments before he died, Jesus spoke the words that changed history: "It is finished" (John 19:30, NIV). On a cruel Roman cross, just outside the Jerusalem gates, the Son of God offered the only atoning sacrifice acceptable for the redemption of all mankind: he offered himself. "By one sacrifice he has made perfect forever those who are being made holy" (Hebrews 10:14, NIV).

As Jesus breathed his final breath, "the veil of the temple was torn in two" (Matthew 27:51, NAS). This indicated the full restoration of mankind's unlimited access to God's presence. The separation that came about in the Garden was reversed. Unbroken connection with God became ours once again. Just as a bridegroom lifts the veil of his beloved bride to symbolize that nothing further separates them from intimate union, "we all, with unveiled face, beholding the glory of the Lord, are being transformed into the same image" (2 Corinthians 3:18, ESV). Through the gift of redemption, we are now unified with God in likeness and righteousness, raised with him in resurrection life, empowered by him for kingdom partnership, and made complete in eternal glory.

Everything I Have Is Yours

Ultimately, we will enjoy this union with *glorified bodies* in an everlasting Garden of Eden paradise. But we're invited to partake in such a glorious alignment on this side of heaven also, for God's delight, our own fulfillment, and for the sake of the world he loves.

Now that we're reunited, our wonderful Source and Savior, the King of kings longs to share his royal treasure with his beloved bride. He desires to bless his people with priceless and extravagant gifts. These gifts include his perfect righteousness, unlimited provision, and the attributes and anointing of the Holy Spirit. "Everything I have is yours" (Luke 15:31, NIV). Once we're reconnected to our vital life Source and have experienced our own "homecoming reunion," we're then sent forth in power to tell every person who is looking for "home" that there is an easy way back.

Jesus said,

> *The Spirit of the Lord is upon me, because he has anointed me to proclaim good news to the poor. He has sent me to proclaim freedom for the prisoners and recovery of sight to the blind, to set the oppressed free, to proclaim the year of the Lord's favor.*

Luke 4:18, NIV —

The calling of Christ's bride is to be empowered and vitalized by the Holy Spirit to accomplish these same works. "I tell you the truth, anyone who believes in me will do the same works I have done, and even greater works, because I am going to be with the Father" (John 14:12, NLT). God has "blessed us with every spiritual blessing" (Ephesians 1:3, NLT) to ensure that this can be so. The same power that worked effectively through Jesus to accomplish miracles and demonstrate grace is ours for the receiving. "His divine power has granted to us all things that pertain to life and godliness, through the knowledge of him who called us to his own glory and excellence" (2 Peter 1:3, ESV).

We've been called to know God in intimate likeness, effective partnership, and unity of purpose. We've been called to nothing less than the Almighty Creator's glory and excellence. It is time for us to identify our strengths and acknowledge the good things that are in us. It is time for us to redefine our passions and streamline our purposes. It is time for us to connect to the vitalizing power of the Holy Spirit by recognizing and believing: all separation between God and man has been extirpated, rescinded, and annulled. "Everything is possible for the one who believes" (Mark 9:23, NIV).

It is time to arise.

It is time to live in your vitality.

Reflections

6
Put On Your Strength

Jilted Lover

I must have blacked out when my head slammed into the living room wall. For a brief moment, everything went dark. Regaining vision, I saw Danielle's tear-filled eyes confronting me with feverish fury. There seemed to be no sense to her actions. How could I have misjudged her character so poorly? I knew she'd had a troubled childhood, but I never imagined she would become violent.

Her uncompromising hands pinned my shoulders to the wall. "What's wrong with you?" I asked, terrified. "Why are you doing this?" Apparently, those weren't the wisest questions to ask. Her right hand moved to my throat as she glared at me threateningly. "You've ruined my life!" she spat venomously. "I want you to love me, and only me!" Bewildered, I tried to make sense of her words. When I agreed to move into her London digs, she *had* seemed overly enthusiastic, and her clingy tendencies were concerning to say the least. Nevertheless, I hadn't noticed any signs of a fragile temper. But when she found out I'd reunited with an old boyfriend, all hell broke loose. Instead of being excited for me, she reacted to the news like a jilted lover. I did the math and realized she must have hidden affections for me beyond those of a typical roommate.

"You're acting crazy! Please stop this!" I screamed. But at the hearing of my words, she wrapped her sweaty fingers all the more tightly around my neck. Her eyes burned into mine with an eerie combination of rage and rejection. I flailed at her arm to shove it away, struggling to free myself from her grip on my throat, but she retaliated by shoving me into the wall. If she was going to "lose" me, it seemed Danielle was determined it would be by her own doing and not mine. As I looked into her disturbed eyes, I realized I was in a fight for my life.

Escape

Danielle was more athletic than me, muscular and strong. Despite her obvious physical advantage, a force of strength suddenly rose up within me—a strength I didn't know I had. Determination must have flashed across my eyes. When she saw it, she tightened her grip on my throat making it difficult for me to breathe. With an almighty surge of effort, I slammed my fist down on her arm and broke free. Taking advantage of her momentary loss of power, I slipped out from under the hand that pinned me to the wall. Then I bolted for the stairs to escape.

She started to chase after me, but something stopped her in her tracks. She stood there, paralyzed, clinging to the staircase, screaming obscenities at me as I tumbled out of the doorway. Terrified, I ran halfway down the street before stopping to look back. In the light of a street lamp, I doubled over to catch my breath trying to make sense of what had just happened. Fortunately, my flat key and travel card were in my back pocket, so I made my way in the rain to a safer place. On a day when I knew she wouldn't be at the flat, I went back to collect my things. Danielle and I never crossed paths again.

Feats of Strength

It didn't help that all this happened just a short while after my first love dropped me off on the side of the road and drove away without so much as a backward glance; I was only just getting back on my feet. Nevertheless, strength to overcome in such a traumatizing situation was there when I needed it, as it is for all of us in our times of greatest need.

Coming close to being choked to death was truly terrifying, but the lesson I learned from the experience is this: Danielle's grip around my throat was tight, but destiny held me even tighter. It wasn't my time to go. Destiny is jealous and unyielding; it stirs within us the strength to overcome, even in the severest of circumstances. It refuses to give us up.

It wasn't long after the perilous incident with Danielle that I booked my flight to America. My intention had been to take a four-month sabbatical to enjoy a season of rest and self-discovery, but the transatlantic trip ended up leading to so much more. Just two nights after my arrival in California, I attended an event that dramatically changed my life.

My host, Francis, invited me to go with her to see The Power Team—a popular group of Christian motivational speakers who performed incredible feats of strength. We arrived early to get a good view, but everyone seemed to have the same idea. Thirty minutes after the doors opened, every seat in the auditorium was taken. Expectation and excitement filled the air for the next hour, and by the time the event got underway the atmosphere was electric. The leader of The Power Team, John Jacobs, talked about God's desire to break chains of addiction and oppression off of people's lives. As he spoke, the bodybuilders broke baseball bats over their legs and snapped handcuffs off their wrists. They rolled up frying pans with their bare hands and tore full-sized telephone books in half. I found myself gasping in awe as I watched. They put on a terrific show that captured the attention of the entire crowd.

Decision

As I stood marveling at the unusual feats of strength demonstrated by these muscular giants, my heart also marveled at their declarations. My own life was unquestionably in chains. My list of wrongdoings was lengthy enough to fill a phone book. I had been burned more than once in life's frying pan of troubles, and too often, I felt like a baseball bat had whacked me upside the head emotionally. Although the message they preached was unfamiliar to me, the visual imagery of their tours de force helped me better understand the good news they conveyed. Quietly in my seat, I began to wonder if the delivering power they spoke of was real.

As I joined in with the crowd to cheer the team on, I made a private decision: at an opportune time during my stay in America, I would talk to the God these fearless men spoke of, and I would ask him to set me free. I desperately needed a Savior in my life. I figured if Jesus *was* real—if he *was* strong enough to help me (as these men had promised), I would finally taste the peace I longed for. My opportune moment came sooner than expected. That very night during the closing prayer, I felt propelled to get out of my seat and walk to the altar. There, amongst hundreds of strangers, I held out my broken heart to God and received his gift of new life. Immediately, I began to experience a peace I had never known before, and in those moments, my spirit was reborn.

Be Strong

Just like the men in the Power Team, I had devoted many years of my life to developing physical strength for sport or performance. Now, after being born again, I was to commence a different kind of training program—this time, to build *spiritual* strength and endurance.

The Word of God commands us to "be strong in the Lord and in the strength of his might" (Ephesians 6:10, ESV). "Be strong" in the original Greek refers to the ongoing process of building strength—a process that happens naturally as we exercise the strength we have. As any fitness instructor will confirm, the principles of endurance and resistance training are clear: If we want our muscles to grow bigger and stronger, we must push them to the "tearing point." After tearing, the muscle fibers repair, but larger and stronger than they were before. It is in this way that strength is built. And similarly, so it is in the building of spiritual, psychological, and emotional strength.

Spiritual Muscle

When our emotional and psychological strength is tested in life's trials, we feel stretched to our limit on every level. It's as though our spiritual muscles reach their capacity and "tear" under the pressure of our circumstances. This tearing often feels like distress or despair, fear or anxiety. During times like these, we must increase our spiritual "protein intake" by feeding on the meat and milk of God's Word. In doing so, we'll experience God's compassionate repair and essential nourishment for our souls. The torn places of our hearts and minds will be healed and we'll experience considerable spiritual growth.

Regardless of our starting point, if we exercise the spiritual muscle we have, we'll become stronger. If we make good use of the "training opportunities" given to us during challenging seasons, our spiritual strength will increase and we'll become better equipped to deal with each new trial that comes our way. It's through this process that we build godly character and become a positive influence for others.

It's worth mentioning that the words "be strong" are also linked to the idea of rest. In a physical training program, it's important to include rest days. Rest days give our muscles a chance to repair and grow after repeated sessions of strenuous exercise. In the same way, it's important for us to regularly lay down the "weights" of our troubles and cares. We do this by giving our heavy burdens to God in prayer. In exchange, we receive his tender comfort so that our weary hearts can be revived.

Partnership

Before I was even aware of God's presence in my life, his strength was in operation. As I exercised my will to live during my terrifying encounter with Danielle, God's saving power and vigor moved through me and I was able to escape from harm. When we reach the end of our own natural capacity, the supernatural strength of God is there to carry us. It's a partnership; we do our best and the Spirit does the rest.

A wonderful example of God's partnership with man is the story of Gideon in Judges chapter 6. In the midst of Israel's fight for freedom from the Midianites, Gideon felt abandoned by God. He poured out his heart in complaint, but the Lord's response was this:

> *"Go in the strength you have and save Israel out of Midian's hand. Am I not sending you?" "Pardon me, my lord," Gideon replied, "but how can I save Israel? My clan is the weakest in Manasseh, and I am the least in my family." The Lord answered, "I will be with you."*
>
> Judges 6:14–16, NIV —

Maybe, like Gideon, you sometimes feel like you're the weakest, the least able, or the most inadequate. It's important for us to know that the same encouragement God gave to Gideon is still being offered to us today: "Go in the strength you have. I will be with you!" God strengthened and empowered Gideon, and with an army of only three hundred men, he won a mighty victory over the Midianite enemy. Always remember: you plus God is a winning majority.

Become Mighty

As we learned in the previous chapter, a biblical hero who understood how to operate in God's power was David. One of the most challenging times in David's life was when the Amalekite army burned down his town and took the women and children captive. The people in David's village blamed him for the assault. In their anger, they spoke of stoning him to death. But David "strengthened himself in the Lord his God" (1 Samuel 30:6, NASB). He later went on to defeat the Amalekite army and rescue the imprisoned women and children. David knew that encouraging himself in the Lord was something he'd have to practice his entire life, even as the King of Israel. It's imperative we learn to do the same.

The meaning of the word *strengthened* in this verse is extensive. The Hebrew word for *strengthened* is *chazaq*. It's a word linked to the idea of binding, fastening upon, establishing, and making firm. It's a word with an attitude, and that attitude is described as "obstinate, valiant, and withstanding." *Strengthen* (in Hebrew) literally means to "*be* recovered" and to "*become* mighty." It's a choice followed by an action.

Haggard

Around the time I was hitting an all-time low emotionally, my body came crashing down too. It's not surprising—studies show that there's a huge correlation between emotional strength and physical well-being. The brokenness in my body was an outward reflection of the brokenness in my soul—brokenness that had been brought about by years of hidden trauma. Though still only entering middle age, I felt washed-up, messed up, and very creaky.

Everything ached—my back, hips, knees, feet—everything! My digestion was out of whack, and my joints felt like they needed a thorough dowsing with 3-in-One oil. Headaches, even migraines, were a daily challenge. Though I'm not a fan of pharmaceutical drugs, I was regularly taking ibuprofen just to manage the pain.

I'd gained weight and my face looked haggard. I couldn't remember the last time I'd worked out. On top of what I call "occupational plate spinning"—a chaotic combination of full-time work, homeschooling, traveling, speaking engagements, taking care of my family, and daily household responsibilities—I was also spinning my wheels trying to bury the brokenness I felt obligated to hide, especially in my line of public ministry work. It took more energy to contain the pain than to express it, but at the time, stuffing it away seemed like my only option. Needless to say, this repression of trauma throughout the years had a harrowing effect on my physical health.

Endurance

All my symptoms seemed to suggest that I needed more rest, but to my surprise, that wasn't in God's recipe for my recovery. I was burning the candle at both ends and longed to work fewer hours. My boss, however, wasn't keen on the idea. I was struggling to keep going and felt like I was falling apart at the seams.

It was then that I heard God speak to me from Hebrews 10:36 (NKJV): "You have need of endurance," he said. I was incredulous. "I have need of *endurance*! God, what are you thinking? I'm exhausted! I think what you mean is, I have need of rest, right?" Again, his words came firmly into my spirit: "Michele, you have need of endurance. It's time for you to strengthen yourself, body, soul, and spirit."

God's heart for our physical health is voiced in 3 John 1:2 (NLT): "I hope all is well with you and that you are as healthy in body as you are strong in spirit." The idea of adding an exercise program to my already crammed schedule seemed absurd, but I knew better than to disregard such clear divine instructions. Apparently, I needed to step out of my comfort zone and put on strength. I was being called to "become mighty" and "be recovered."

The Plan

I began with my diet. Aware that food allergies were potentially the cause of many of my day-to-day ailments, I refined my meals to vegetables, fruits, and lean proteins, and avoided processed foods containing additives and preservatives. My digestive system improved within a few weeks. The headaches decreased also. I started playing tennis and did workout DVDs at home. Despite my athletic background, I found the weight training exercises challenging, but I pressed on, confident that the workouts would seem easier as time went by.

Within four months, my previously stiff and aching joints began to feel rejuvenated. I had more energy than I'd had in a long time, and even dropped two dress sizes. I was able to see that regular exercise along with a healthy diet could help me maintain a more positive outlook on life. And I discovered it really is true: when we use the strength we have, more is added.

The parallels between physical and spiritual capacity are profound. Strength and endurance are developed through a willingness to stick things out. They're built through an unyielding commitment to never give up, even in the face of discomfort and pain. When I first embarked on a wellness journey, I didn't enjoy the discomforts of physical challenge, but little did I know, these strength-building disciplines would later help save my life. God had foreseen that I was about to encounter a daunting season of physical illness and emotional distress. There was a chance I might not have endured to victory had I not been adequately strengthened in advance.

India

India is not for the fainthearted; it's an overwhelming place to be if all you've ever known is a comfortable, sanitary, western existence.

When an opportunity came my way to minister in Mumbai, I did not take it lightly. I was aware that my physical constitution was far from hardy, but the opportunity to partner with influential leaders in such an impoverished city was of keen importance to me. While there, I availed myself to be a blessing in whatever ways were most useful to our hosts. This included leading workshops and creative arts training sessions. Additionally, to my delight, on our team's final day in the city, I was asked to speak at an evangelistic event for a large slum dwelling community. About one thousand precious men, women, and children attended the gathering held that same night in a large, run-down building.

At the close of the service, the entire throng crowded around the ministry team and me. Though the sea of precious souls owned few material goods, it was obvious they were rich in faith. One by one, they came forward requesting prayer for themselves and their families. In tearful desperation, many of the women grabbed my hands and placed them on the heads of their feverish, sick children. Doctors and medicines weren't an option for these needy people. Their only hope for relief was a healing touch from God. After the meeting, the team and I returned to our hotel where we packed up our suitcases for the red-eye flight to London. Within twenty-four hours of departing from Mumbai, I began to feel horribly ill.

Montezuma's Revenge

I suspect I may have ingested some kind of bacteria, virus, or parasite. Whatever it was, it dealt a hefty blow to my newly regained health. A month passed before I could eat normally again, but even then, the ordeal was far from over. Six weeks after my initial recovery, "Montezuma" returned again—this time with a vengeance. It hit me much worse the second time around. I had to visit the bathroom about forty times a day. Restful sleep became a dream since nighttime visits were just as frequent. A mere sip of water would trigger a return. The crippling symptoms continued relentlessly for nine long months.

Absorbing nutrition became a challenge. I realized that had I not built up my strength before the onset of the sickness, its effects would have been even more debilitating. Over the course of the illness, my weight dropped to ninety pounds (which doesn't leave much padding on a five-foot four-inch frame). I was permanently cold to the bone, even during the summertime. I could barely climb up a flight of stairs, and my hair stopped growing. I spent every day sitting lifelessly in a chair. Going out was a recipe for embarrassment. Worst of all, the malnutrition led to brain fog. As the British would say, I felt like death warmed up. Prayers were prayed but nothing changed. None of the doctors I went to could figure out the cause of the sickness. Eventually, I stopped trying to find answers; it was simply too tiring to get up and go out.

Digging Deep

I had no choice but to dig deep for strength at a time when I had little. The fact that a severe relational storm was blowing through my life during the same season made the situation all the more challenging. Desperate thoughts swirled around in my dulled, malnourished mind. The emotional pain seemed too much to bear and I couldn't see any light at the end of the tunnel. Mustering the strength to keep going took everything I had and more.

I realized it was crucial that I establish clear motives for my recovery. I reminded myself that my children needed me and there were creative dreams I wanted to pursue. I worked hard to keep these positive motives at the forefront of my daily focus. I couldn't retain food, so the meat, milk, and bread of God's Word became my nourishment.

I remembered Deuteronomy 8:3 (NIV) that says, "man does not live on bread alone but on every word that comes from the mouth of the Lord." I began to devour the promises of God and intentionally feast on hope. Resilient faith began to build within me. Little by little it displaced my fear that I might never be well again. I declared often, "with his stripes we are healed" (Isaiah 53:5, ASV), and trusted that the higher truth of God's Word would ultimately trump facts.

Putting on Strength

In my emaciated, rag doll condition, I struggled to grow strong in body, but I dared to grow strong in faith. Romans 4:17 says God "calls those things which are not as though they are" (Jubilee Bible 2000). He "calls into being that which does not exist" (NASB) and "creates new things out of nothing" (NLT). Even though I knew a full recovery might yet take a while to manifest, I chose to partner with God in the faith-filled creative process of calling things that are not as though they are. I began visualizing myself as healthy and well again, touching the world with the message of God's unconditional love.

Each day, despite feeling fragile, I obeyed the command: "Put on your strength" (Isaiah 52:1, NKJV). I thought of myself as a female Clark Kent, clothed in God's cape of might, exchanging my human frailty for his supernatural power. This imagery might seem far-fetched, but it helped get me through one of the most physically challenging seasons of my life.

Surpassing Power

When David strengthened himself in the Lord during his trial with the Amalekites, he exercised his faith to "be recovered" and to "become mighty." His behavior was a contradiction to his circumstances, but it was perfectly aligned with "the surpassing greatness of his power toward us who believe" (Ephesians 1:19, NASB). God's power *surpasses* every challenge we face. It *overtakes* our situation so as to meet our needs. That's why we must never give up!

Some might describe "putting on strength" as fabricated—fake— trying to be something we're not. Obviously, if we're bedridden, we shouldn't try to run a marathon, but calling things that are not as though they are and strengthening ourselves by using the strength we have is the act of becoming *who we already are* in the finished work of the Savior: whole, healed, and complete. By activating our spiritual muscles to "become mighty," "behave valiantly," and "put on strength," we *will* grow stronger in spirit.

Strong in Faith

Thousands of years ago, Abraham, the father of faith, related to God with an understanding of his "unpronounceable name"— YHWH (sometimes written and read as "Yahweh"). The full meaning of this all-inclusive name of God isn't crystal clear, but scholars agree its meaning includes: *Life-giver, Creator, and the one bringing into being—he who brings to pass—the one who is a performer of his promises—the one who will approve himself and give evidence of his being—the absolute and unchangeable one—the ever-living one who is ever coming into manifestation, and the one who was, who is, and will be.* Wow! These characteristics of God are inspiring!

God promised Abraham a son—an heir that would come from his own body, even in his old age. Abraham was seventy-five years old when the promise was given, and one hundred years old when Isaac was born. Abraham's wife, Sarah, was also well past childbearing age. Considering the amazing characteristics of YHWH, it's not difficult to see why Abraham remained steadfast in his faith: "With respect to the

promise of God, he did not waver in unbelief but grew strong in faith...
fully assured that what God had promised, he was able also to perform"
(Romans 4:20–21, NASB). Abraham knew that God is the "one who is
ever coming into manifestation"—"the Creator and the giver of life."
As recipients of new covenant blessings, we have the opportunity for
the presence and power of the Holy Spirit to dwell within us. When the
Spirit of God lives in us, his characteristics and qualities reside within
us also. How much more then should we not fully trust God to give
evidence of who he is in our lives? How much more should we not fully
believe in his ability to provide for our every need?

Logical Choice

The physical challenges I went through following my trip to Mumbai
can't in any way be compared to the immense trials of cancer patients
or those suffering with painful illnesses, debilitating handicaps,
and life-threatening diseases. But regardless of the severity of our
circumstances, the same wisdom applies: fixing our eyes on the Author
and Finisher of our faith is far more productive than fixing them on our
circumstances. Like Abraham, we must make a firm decision to look to
the one who gives us strength. We must steadfastly refuse to become
weak in faith.

In my spirit, I knew it wasn't my time to die. I was also aware of the
reality of an unseen spiritual enemy whose mission is to steal, kill, and
destroy. His plan was to shut me down and prevent me from carrying
out my purpose. My only logical choice, therefore, was to believe
for a full recovery, regardless of how things looked. I continued to
strengthen myself to the best of my ability and trusted God to do the
rest.

In the fullness of time, the mystery illness finally came to an end.
I really can't identify any one specific moment that led to the turning

point in my road to recovery, nor do I have an explanation as to why it took so long for the symptoms to dissipate. But I'm truly grateful for the spiritual muscle that was built within me during that season of waiting and endurance. I underwent an extensive internal renovation during that time also. I felt like I was at ground zero in every area of my life, but God was faithful to create new things out of nothing. Though I was weak, I became strong (Joel 3:10, KJV). I was living proof that his "power is perfected in weakness" (2 Corinthians 12:9, NASB). When we surrender to God in times of need and put our focus on his empowering presence, God's strength rushes in to fill up the empty places in our souls. The greater our emptiness and hunger for God, the more of his strength we are able to experience.

Patient Endurance

There are some levels of internal strength that can *only* be built through waiting. And I don't mean the flicking-through-magazines-at-the-checkout type of waiting. The Hebrew definition of *wait* involves "binding together" with the Lord. It's an attitude of patient endurance coupled with confident expectation. "Now hope does not disappoint, because the love of God has been poured out in our hearts" (Romans 5:5, NKJV). "Wait on the Lord: be of good courage, and he shall strengthen your heart" (Psalm 27:14, AKJV).

Endurance training through waiting builds the heart strength we need for confidence, influence, and productivity in the seasons of our lives that are about to unfold. There may be areas of our character that require adjustment before we move into fulfillments of promise. A season of waiting is a great time to make those much-needed adjustments. It's a time to "let endurance have its perfect result, so that you may be perfect and complete, lacking in nothing" (James 1:4, NASB).

Anointing

It's our fullness of spirit that internally sustains us when we're going through trials and challenges. When my body was emaciated with sickness, the fullness of God within me kept me alive. In fact, Ephesians 1:23 (NIV) describes the church as "his body, his fullness." God is watching over his own body—his church—his bride—to protect her and care for her. "That's why we are not discouraged. No, even if outwardly we are wearing out, inwardly we are being renewed each and every day" (2 Corinthians 4:16, NIV).

I'm all for staying trim and healthy, but there's a fatness and fullness I definitely don't want to miss out on. It's a fatness of *spirit* that destroys yokes of bondage. The word *fatness* (*shemen* in the original Hebrew) can be interchanged with the word "oil" or "anointing." The Messiah, the anointed one, invites us to become immersed in his anointing and filled with the Holy Spirit. In this "fatness" of God's Spirit, debilitating burdens and yokes of bondage fall away. Offenses are unable to stick; when they touch the "oil" of God's anointing, it's as though they slip right off.

Attempting to deal with yokes of bondage through outwardly enforced behavior management only ever yields temporary results. The best way to deal with bondage of any kind is from the inside out. When we allow our hearts to be filled with God's presence, power, and purposes, the law of displacement kicks into action. The things that no longer belong in our lives lose place to the things that do. The fatness of God's anointing causes yokes of slavery to bust right off our necks. "The yoke shall be destroyed because of the anointing" (Isaiah 10:27, KJV). "The yoke will be torn away because you have grown fat" (Isaiah 10:27, GWT).

Special Occasion

In place of yokes of bondage, we're to be adorned with "garments of splendor" and "beautiful clothes" (Isaiah 52:1). In day-to-day life, some people prefer to save their good clothes for special occasions. But when it comes to our spiritual attire, God does not have a "save it for best" attitude. *Every* day is our best day in the Kingdom of God. Of course, there may be times when a shoestring budget forces us to be especially careful with our possessions and expenditures, but a poverty mentality should not be applied to God's limitless blessings.

In the natural world, dressing in our best clothes helps us to feel empowered and ready for anything; after all, why would we dress in stained and tattered garments if we have something better to wear? The same philosophy applies to our spiritual attire. Amazing garments have been provided for us, but they are of no benefit if we don't put them on. Isaiah 61:10 (ESV) says "he has clothed me with the garments of salvation; he has covered me with the robe of righteousness." Once received, these garments are not to be removed; they're to be worn permanently. In putting on the garment of salvation and the robe of righteousness, we're clothing ourselves in the permanent security of everlasting life and an assurance of strength that can never be stripped away. Our label will always read "God's Own."

Sealed

A beautiful Dutch woman by the name of Corrie Ten Boom was imprisoned in the Ravensbrück Concentration Camp during World War II for helping Jews escape from the Nazis. One of my favorite quotes of hers is this: "I was five years old when I asked Jesus to come into my heart. He came and he never left." This statement stayed with me from the second I heard it. A solid assurance of salvation such as this is paramount to the out-workings of its power in our lives.

When we trust that all barriers of separation between God and man have been eliminated, God gladly honors that trust. When the power of redemption comes into our hearts, it never leaves. This permanence eradicates deep-rooted fears of rejection and establishes within us a foundation of security that's solid and unshakable. We can rest in the knowledge that we're accepted and welcome in the loving and gracious presence of God.

When the apostle Paul described himself as a "prisoner of the Lord," (Ephesians 4:1) I believe to some degree, he was referring to the seal of the Holy Spirit. Ephesians 1:13 (ISV) says, "When you believed in the Messiah, you were sealed with the promised Holy Spirit, who is the guarantee of our inheritance." A mental image that helps me lay hold of this truth is that of a bowl of food covered and sealed with indestructible, everlasting, extra-strength Cling Wrap. Once sealed, even if the bowl is turned upside down, the contents won't fall out. In the same way, when we believe in Jesus Christ as our Savior, we're sealed forever into God's family and name. No matter how upside-down or shaken up our lives might seem to be, we're captive to the unconditional love of God. We cannot escape his goodness and mercy. How comforting it is to know that we're safely sealed into God's heart of love—past, present, and forever.

Free Gift

One of the greatest spiritual garments we've been given is the robe of righteousness—eternal right standing with God. This righteousness is not something we can earn or buy. It's God's *own* righteousness, given to us a free gift forever. The robe of righteousness is not a removable garment to be taken off when we're "bad" and put back on when we're "good." Righteousness hasn't been given to us only to be taken away again. God's free gift of righteousness doesn't require renewal; it's a permanent lifetime blessing with no return policy.

It *is* possible, however, for our robes to become dirtied through thoughtless actions, rebellious behavior, or scathing indifference to God's grace. But a "supernatural laundry service" has been provided for repentant hearts where even the worst of stains can be cleansed away: "Come now, let's settle this," says the Lord. "Though your sins are like scarlet, I will make them as white as snow. Though they are red like crimson, I will make them as white as wool" (Isaiah 1:18, NLT).

Coat of Strength

In addition to robes of righteousness and salvation, there's another incredible garment we've been given to wear: our mantle—our calling—the tasks and purposes to which we're assigned, along with the gifts, talents, and personality traits we've been given to accomplish them.

The coat of many colors given to Joseph by his father, in Genesis chapter 37, was a type and shadow of just such a mantle. "Now Israel loved Joseph more than any other of his sons, because he was the son of his old age. And he made him a robe of many colors" (Genesis 37:3, ESV). In the same way that Joseph received a unique and colorful coat from his father, we too have received a personalized mantle from our heavenly Father. This mantle is the colorful combination of our personality, characteristics, experience, and abilities. It's our very own custom designed coat of strength given to empower us to fulfill all of our unique potential and destiny.

Joseph wore his coat of strength to honor the one who made it for him, yet Joseph's brothers ridiculed him for it. They knew Joseph's coat represented an irrevocable mantle of blessing and favor, and they despised him because of it, and betrayed him. We too have a responsibility to put on our coat of strength with humble confidence. Yet we should understand that some people will dislike us for standing firm in our personhood to live our lives with bold and colorful enthusiasm.

Never Give Up

Joseph endured many harsh trials along the rocky road to the fulfillment of his dreams. His coat was stripped from him, he was left for dead in a pit of rejection, he was betrayed and forsaken by the family he loved, and he was thrown into prison for a crime he didn't commit. But despite all he went through, Joseph found strength in the God of his dreams.

> *Do you not know? Have you not heard? The everlasting God, the Lord, the creator of the ends of the earth does not become weary or tired. His understanding is inscrutable. He gives strength to the weary, and to him who lacks might he increases power. Though youths grow weary and tired, and vigorous young men stumble badly, yet those who wait for the Lord will gain new strength; they will mount up with wings as eagles, they will run and not get tired, they will walk and not become weary.*
>
> Isaiah 40:28–31, NASB —

God's plan to lead Joseph into his destiny remained certain. After all, it was God who had given Joseph his dreams in the first place. Even "if we are faithless, he remains faithful—for he cannot deny himself" (2 Timothy 2:13, ESV). "For the gifts and the calling of God are irrevocable" (Romans 11:29, NASB). They cannot be shaken off. No matter how severe our trials might be, our God-given calling remains, beating in our hearts, spurring us forward, never allowing us to throw in the towel. We need our coat of strength to help us accomplish the specific tasks and assignments we've been given. No matter how many times our coat of strength is stripped from our backs through jealousy, betrayal, tragedy, struggle, misunderstanding, or tribulation, we need to keep putting it back on again. Relentlessly, fearlessly, and continually, we must put on our strength.

God Idea

On many occasions over the years, I felt as though I reached the end of my own strength and abilities. Yet each time, God stepped in to display his dominion and might on my behalf. One such time was when I left South Africa with my [former] husband in hopes of living permanently in the United States.

The plan sounded great in theory, but we knew obtaining permanent resident visas for the United States would be easier said than done. Nevertheless, we put on the strength we had, activated our faith, poured all of our finances into buying air tickets, and landed back in Los Angeles with our firstborn son. (He was eleven months old at the time.) Temporary visitor visas were stamped into our passports. We were about to find out if attempting to live permanently in America was a good idea or a God idea. If it was a God idea, I was confident a way would be made.

We worked with a wonderful immigration lawyer, but despite all of our efforts over many months, every door remained closed. Our last shot was the Green Card Lottery. The Diversity Visa lottery program originated in the mid-eighties to help increase immigrant entries into the United States from underrepresented countries. The lawyer submitted our entries but solemnly reminded us that the odds of us obtaining a visa were slim. There were over ten million applicants from all over the world, and there would only be forty thousand "winners."

Hold On

Many weeks went by without us hearing any updates. It was a stressful time because we knew that our visitor visas were soon to expire. The idea of going elsewhere seemed impossible. There was barely enough money to buy groceries let alone fly back to England or South Africa. The expected time for the Green Card winners to be announced had come and gone. It was a desperate situation. Without a work visa there was no work, and without work there was no income or food. I felt anxious, but the still, small voice in my heart encouraged me to hold on and not make plans for defeat.

I had no other choice but to strengthen myself in the Lord, behave valiantly, and become mighty. I knew my faith had the potential to become "the substance of things hoped for and the evidence of things not seen" (Hebrews 11:1, KJV). My spiritual muscles were being pushed to their limit. I got down on my knees and cried out to God for whom absolutely nothing is impossible. A few days later, the phone call came. The Green Cards were won! Once again, it became evident: when tenacious faith aligns with destiny purposes, "all things are possible to him who believes!" (Mark 9:23, BSB)

Promised Land

Hearing this great news was, of course, a mighty victory, but there was a downside: We learned that there were many red tape hoops yet to be jumped through before our permanent residency could be considered a done deal. The next stage of the immigration process required us to return to South Africa. This information hit us like a sledgehammer. We had zero income and zero savings. Purchasing air tickets was out of the question. The thought of having gotten this far but not being able to take the final step was crushing. Another miracle was needed and fast!

Once again, I was presented with a chance to build spiritual muscle. There was no other option but to trust in God, and to believe for another demonstration of his power, strength, and dominion on my behalf. I get goose bumps every time I recount how this impossible situation was turned around, but truly, this is what happened: Two weeks after our Green Cards were won, the Los Angeles Department of Immigration and Naturalization changed the processing law! I nearly fell out of my chair when the lawyer explained our case developments. Flying back to South Africa would no longer be required. The paperwork needed to secure our permanent residency would now be processed in California. My little family and I became the first foreigners in West Coast immigration history to finalize the details of our Green Card victory right there in Los Angeles.

This stretching season of geographical upheaval reminded me of God's command to Joshua to "be strong and courageous" (Joshua 1:9, NASB). Because of Joshua's resilience and fortitude, he led Israel's descendants into the land of promise one obedient step at a time. When we're strong and courageous like Joshua, we also will see the fulfillment of our Promised Land dreams. God will make sure his plan for our lives is accomplished. Nothing can prevail against his might and strength.

It's Time

What doesn't kill us really can make us stronger. Psalm 84:5–7 (NLT) reminds us that there's joy to be found in the challenging seasons that cause us to dig deep for strength: "What joy for those whose strength comes from the Lord... when they walk through the Valley of Weeping, it will become a place of refreshing springs... they will continue to grow stronger."

Our valleys of weeping and our adverse conditions can be like boot camp training sessions that force us to exercise the strength we have. The more we do this, the stronger we'll become. We each have a choice: Either we buckle under the pressures of life and give in to weakness and defeat, or we use our challenging circumstances as opportunities to put on strength and build endurance. No matter what we go through, we can be sure of this: We do not face our tests and trials alone but with a heaven-sent coach who never leaves our side. "The Lord is on my side; I will not fear" (Psalm 118:6, KJV). "I can do all things through him who strengthens me" (Philippians 4:13, ESV).

It's time for us to put on strength and overcome those things that would otherwise overcome us. It's time for us to become mighty and behave valiantly. It's time for us to wear our spiritual garments with confidence and boldly call into being things that are not as though they are. Strength is the tenacious force within us that holds us to our course and empowers us to lay hold of our destiny. Let us be strong, therefore, in the power of unlimited might! (Ephesians 6:10)

It is time to arise.

It is time to put on your strength.

Reflections

_____

_____

_____

_____

_____

_____

_____

_____

_____

_____

_____

_____

_____

7
Lift Up Your Voice

Clarity and Peace

The clarity of our voice depends on the certainty of our identity and the ease with which we connect to our own unique personhood. When we know who we are, where we come from, what we're made of, and what we stand for, we're able to speak with confidence and communicate with love. When our convictions are aligned with universal principles and governed by reliable truths, we're able to lift up our voices with wisdom and make a positive, influential difference in our world.

Attaining communicative clarity and confidence can take time. In my teenage years and early twenties, I felt shaky about my identity. I was irresolute about what I really believed and felt a sense of internal emptiness. I studied many religions during that time in an attempt to appease the aching void in my heart. I gleaned some inspiring insights from my studies, but none of them gave me the lasting peace and spiritual lucidity I'd been yearning for since I was a child. Coming up empty-handed again and again was partly what caused me to call out to Jesus for salvation and rescue.

I'm grateful to say that I was still a young woman when I arrived at my first reliable stepping-stones to peace. Life's unpleasant realities had ushered me to a place of acknowledgement that I needed a savior to help me bridge the gap from this world to the next. Light and truth broke through to help me understand that there was nothing I could do to get myself "back to Eden"—back to a place of completeness, security, and oneness with God, both now and after death. In that realization, I settled it that I could not redeem myself. I recognized that the only one qualified to help me was "the lamb of God, who takes away the sin of the world" (John 1:29, NASB).

Though separated from the power of redemption for the first twenty-four years of my life, Jesus's perfect, atoning sacrifice *had already* bridged the gap; I just needed to receive it and align my beliefs with the security and freedom he'd effected on my behalf. When at last my life was aligned with saving grace, a divine peace that surpasses all understanding became mine. It still guards my heart and mind to this day.

Certainty

Eternal peace can only become ours when we exchange our own attempts at right standing with God for the gift of his perfect righteousness. Ephesians 2:8 (ISV) says "this gift does not come from you. It is the gift of God." First John 5:13 (NIV) comforts us saying, "I write these things to you who believe in the name of the Son of God so that you may know that you have eternal life." It *is* possible for us to *know* that we have eternal life—to be absolutely certain of it.

Eternal life is more than a length of time; it's a quality of life filled with peace and joy, saturated in the light and love of the Creator. The Bible, God's love letter of promise, tells us how to walk in the assurance of eternal life. But such confident assurance does not become ours by luck or by chance. The gift of eternal life has been provided, but it must be received. Once it is received, the deepest of all our concerns—that of life after death—will be reconciled in our hearts.

We simply need to take a moment in time—maybe even right now—to reconnect to the abundant, eternal life available to us through Christ's redemption. Once we've accepted God's gift and peace becomes ours, we'll begin to understand the indescribable value of the gospel message—a message we're called to share with everyone we meet.

If you haven't received God's gifts of righteousness and eternal life—if you haven't asked Jesus to redeem you back to your completeness and oneness with God—simply reach your heart out to the Savior with these simple words:

"Jesus, I accept your redeeming sacrifice and I welcome

the Spirit's presence fully into my life. Thank you that I
am awakened and restored to my unlimited potential—
connected to Love's everlasting Source and the essence of
my true being."

Having come into alignment with the omnipotent, omniscient, omnipresent life force, we are "made complete with all the fullness of life and power that comes from God" (Ephesians 3:19, NLT). In this completeness, "everything is possible for one who believes" (Mark 9:23, NIV). In this fullness, we have peace knowing that we're connected to the power that is "our refuge and strength, always ready to help in times of trouble" (Psalm 46:1, ESV). Not only that, but we're connected to the power by which our hearts' desires and purposes are fulfilled. (Psalm 20:4)

As we take delight in this awesome power, our desires and purposes will materialize and manifest. (Psalm 37:4) In contrast, when we "bite into" a negative mindset of "not enough" (like Adam and Eve did in the Garden), we create unnecessary resistance to God's readily available goodness, and "fall short" of the things we're intended to experience and enjoy. This is why we're instructed to "have no other gods before me" (Exodus 20:3, ISV). These gods of blockage and resistance show up in many forms such as negative thoughts and communication, doubt, unbelief, and perspectives that focus on our apparent "reality" of lack. How glorious it is to know that we've been restored to oneness with the Creator of the universe. The largest, truest component of who we are now has the potential for continual partnership with God to ask, expect, and receive all the good things that have already been prepared beforehand for us to walk in. (Ephesians 2:10, ESV)

Not Ashamed

When it comes to lifting up our voices to share the good news of redemption, it's essential we be fully persuaded of the message on our lips. Under the pervasive pressures of religious or evolutionary mindsets, we might be tempted to temper our words in an empathetic desire to be relevant. I'm all for being all things to all men, but it's important that we differentiate between relevance and impotence. In the name of relevance, we must be careful not to water down the message of redemption to the degree that it becomes an impotent mixture.

We need to draw a line in our own hearts, settle our convictions, and boldly lift up our voices to declare, "I'm not ashamed of the Good News. It is God's power to save everyone who believes" (Romans 1:16, GWT). If the good news we share is to be well received, it's imperative that our communication be in alignment with the motive of the gospel—love. "For God so loved the world that he gave his one and only Son" (John 3:16, NIV). If our communication is judgmental, dogmatic, and scathing, we can only expect to reap what we sow. Whether inwardly or outwardly, spoken or unspoken, our words will reap after their kind—judgment for judgment, hatred for hatred, alienation for alienation, or love for love.

If we focus on verbalizing what we're against rather than what we're for, we're in danger of misrepresenting the heart of God to the world he loves, especially if our opinions are laced with condemnation. John 3:17 (GWT) says, "God sent his Son into the world, not to condemn the world, but to save the world." We've been admonished: "do not let any unwholesome talk come out of your mouths, but only what is helpful for building others up according to their needs, that it may benefit those who listen" (Ephesians 4:29, NIV).

Words Matter

One of the best ways to build people up is to first listen to what they have to say. By "tuning in" to people's needs, we're better positioned to respond with genuine compassion and informed concern. Communication is like sowing seed. With every seed sown, there will be a harvest reaped. We're not responsible for the soil into which our "word seeds" are planted, but we are responsible for the quality of the seeds we sow. If we don't have something good to say, it's better that we hold our tongue. Words can be like medicine or poison, truth or lies. They can strengthen or destroy, encourage or break down. Whichever way we look at it, our words are never neutral; there *will* be a reaping for the words we sow. Lifting up our voices with life-giving communication requires self-control, but the reward certainly makes the effort worthwhile. As rabbis throughout the centuries have so wisely said, "He who blesses is blessed!"

Words matter. We could even say they *are* matter! At the most basic level, our words are a form of creative energy, (as are our thoughts and feelings); they are substance without form. If you've ever walked into a room where people are arguing and tearing each other down with their words, you will understand what I mean. Even if the volume were muted, the discomfort felt by the negative energy would make you want to vacate the area. The converse is also true. Wherever people are laughing and enjoying each other's company, extending love and speaking with kindness, the atmosphere is comfortable. The energy in the room is welcoming. It makes you want to pull up a chair and join in the fun. Communication is more powerful than we might realize. Whether verbalized or unspoken, our thoughts, words, and body language create the environment in which we live.

Snapshot

Lifting up our voices can take many forms, but making a positive difference starts in our hearts. Matthew 12:34 says, "The mouth speaks out of that which fills the heart" (NASB); "Whatever is in your heart determines what you say" (NLT). Ultimately, that which is in our hearts will show up in our words, as well as in the tone of our voice, our body language, and the motives behind our communication. Knowing this, it behooves us to cleanse our hearts daily from a buildup of hurts and frustrations that can so rapidly be accrued. Like hot lava bubbling in a volcano, our pent-up negative sentiments have the potential to erupt during times of stress and scald the poor souls who are misfortunate enough to be caught in their volatile pathway.

If we want a revealing snapshot of our hearts, it's helpful to listen to the conversations we have with ourselves and with others. In doing so, we're likely to discover what we really feel and believe. The fruit of our thoughts, words, and actions are evidenced in our relationships and circumstances as an expression and reflection of our heart's beliefs in any given situation. Where there's frustration, disconnection, discord, and passive-aggressive exchange, it's likely that negative core beliefs are at the root, as well as the repression of emotions or the projection of fears cultivated by prior adverse experiences. Unless these negative core beliefs are intercepted and replaced, they have the tendency to perpetuate damaging twists on truth through unproductive communication.

Nuisance

Many years ago, I was asked to be a guest speaker for an evening session at a three-day conference in California. On the second day of the conference, my work colleague and I met for coffee in the hotel lobby to talk about the next day's itinerary. I reiterated that I was hoping to skip the breakfast session so that I could meet a deadline on a writing assignment. I'd been assured that my personal plans would not create any inconvenience for the conference hosts, yet once again, I found myself asking anxiously, "Do you *really* think it's okay? I'm worried they'll be irritated about having to pick me up at a different time? I don't want to be a burden." "There you go again," my colleague said with a wink, "thinking of yourself as a disturbance and a nuisance—apologizing for your very existence."

I stopped dead in my tracks as these jovial, but confronting, words sank in. Aside from the fact that they revealed a very British side to my personality, they exposed within me a core belief that had been buried in my heart since childhood—a core belief that had prevented me from boldly lifting up my voice even in the face of personal abuse or mistreatment. It was the belief (or fear) that if I spoke up for myself over a personal need, I would be considered an inconvenience to the people around me, and therefore, unwelcome, and likely to be tossed aside. (How this core belief was first formed in my heart is described in chapter three.)

Right Alignment

The admonishment I received from my colleague that day was something I'd heard before, but this time, it really hit home. The moment had come for me to acknowledge my "truth"—the belief that having my personal needs met equated with the idea that I was a nuisance to people.

There that day in the hotel lobby, I saw an example of how our thought patterns and communication often align with our subconscious perspectives. I had uncovered what some psychologists refer to as a "pain cycle"—an emotionally painful or destructive behavior pattern rooted in a negative core belief. In my case, a subtle fear of rejection was prompting a cycle of keep-your-mouth-shut, man-pleasing behaviors with a subconscious goal to stay in people's good books. It perpetuated within me a sense that I did not quite belong—that I was tolerated but not really wanted.

In reality, of course, people rarely considered me a nuisance for making my needs known, but when I insisted on spluttering self-depreciating apologies out of a belief that I was, there was a much higher chance they'd end up agreeing with me. And there would be the evidence my subconscious was looking for in order to prove that my belief was correct. (Our minds always do what they believe we want them to do—they always act in accordance with our strongest repetitive thoughts and core beliefs.) Thanks to my colleague, who spoke the truth to me in love, the lights came on and I saw the pattern. There and then, it was time to replace my warped core belief with truth, and align my thoughts and words accordingly from that moment forward.

Genuine Transformation

It's important to note that we "play into" our pain cycles and the avoidance of discomfort because our minds are hardwired to pursue pleasure. In short, we tend to do whatever it takes to avoid (re) experiencing pain and discomfort associated with unpleasant memories of rejection, abandonment, neglect, etc. We tend to sidetrack this discomfort by taking what we feel is the easiest route of avoidance (though only ever temporary) such as medicating and masking our pain or employing all manners of behavior management tactics.

We have to understand that pain cycles are the "stuck" places in our development—the unresolved experiences from our past that keep us from intimacy, confidence, and security in the present. They are one of the most valuable weapons in Satan's arsenal to keep us from the truth of our empowerment in God. They are the blindfolds that prevent us from seeing and internalizing the completeness of love that's been restored to us though redemption.

Genuine transformation takes place when we renew our minds by "taking every thought captive to obey Christ" (2 Corinthians 10:5, HCSB). It's essential that we do this if we want to create a better experience for ourselves in the present. But because our minds are inclined to repeat familiar patterns, it takes focused effort to "capture" our thoughts and replace them with higher truth. To reprogram our unproductive thoughts and words, it's helpful to trace them back to the negative core beliefs from which they derive. Once those negative core beliefs are illumined, they can be "reset." New beliefs can be written on our hearts according to our true identity so that healthy thoughts and communication can flourish from that time on.

In my example, a core belief was revealed—a belief that I was potentially a nuisance to people—tolerated but not fully accepted (especially when vocalizing a personal request). Through earnest thought, and with the help of the Holy Spirit, I traced the origin of that negative belief back to my childhood. Several "scenes" came to mind from my past—times when I'd been unduly judged, reprimanded, or shamed for using my voice or speaking up for myself. I "watched the scenes" through my mind's eye and connected to the anguish I felt all those years ago. I re-ran history in my conscious soul knowing that I was now empowered to intelligently resolve the outcome of each incident by creating a new perspective with my older, wiser eyes and heart.

I made a conscious choice to differentiate between the emotionally intelligent woman that I am today and the deep-rooted wounds that had perpetuated my ongoing negative thought patterns. I forgave the people who'd hurt me, and recognized that, whether out of ignorance or malicious intent, they had behaved according to the limited understanding they had at the time. In my redeemed power, I wiped the slate clean, left the past where it belonged, and prepared to write a new script for the present and future.

Default Response

Having revisited the past to recognize when, how, and where a fear of disapproval became rooted in my heart, it was time to allow transformation to take place. My next step was to find the specific word that most resonated with my negative experiences from the past. "Rejected" was the word that most accurately described how I felt when disdained for articulating a need.

The fear of rejection is a common pain cycle that's rooted in an even *deeper* layer of belief—the belief that we are "not enough." If deep down in our souls we believe we're not worthy of acceptance and unconditional love, we tend to fall into the subconscious snare of doing whatever we perceive is necessary to avoid the pain of rejection, even if those actions are dishonoring to ourselves or to others. Alternatively, we will keep a wall up over our hearts to ensure that we never run the risk of experiencing rejection. (This is often the pattern for those who've been exposed to the agony of unwanted separation in their formative years.)

In displacing pain cycles, it's crucial we grasp the information contained in chapter three of this book—that our value is incalculable, and that we've been redeemed from death and unworthiness (*mwuth*) to union with God in likeness and completeness (*d'mwuth*). Without a fundamental outworking of redemption in our lives, we are likely to fall prey to the same delusion that bewitched Adam and Eve—the lie that our true, authentic self is not enough and that we're unworthy of the goodness we're meant to experience!

New Patterns

My next step towards transformation was to identify my typical "default" responses during the times I felt afraid of being rejected. I recognized that anxiety, withdrawal, and insecurity were typical responses for me—cycles of pain that were still being acted out decades after the events that initially formed my negative core belief. I saw clearly how these default responses played out in my thoughts, communication, and actions (as was apparent with my colleague that day in the hotel lobby).

As with all obsolete programs, there's a time to replace the ones that repeatedly cause glitches. It was time for me to delete the old cycle and "download" a new program—a new belief—one that was rooted in love (not fear) and aligned to the truth of redemption. I sought for a word that resonated in my heart by which to establish a *new core belief*. The word I chose was "welcome." In the eyes of my heavenly Father, I'm not a disappointment for being who I am. I am not in constant threat of disapproval and rejection—none of us are. As God's redeemed children, we are *welcome and accepted*. We are welcome, wanted, and enough.

Since that transformational moment, whenever I've been confronted with the fear of rejection (identifiable by default responses of anxiety, withdrawal, and insecurity), I've reiterated to myself my new core belief: "When I communicate my needs, I am not a nuisance; I am welcomed, wanted, and enough." By internalizing the truth of that statement through repetition and application, my formerly negative pattern shifted to a positive perspective that I've carried in my heart ever since.

On the most part, I regularly experience this elevated reality. But if I run into situations where there's intolerance for my needs, I am confidently able to create boundaries or confront the issues at hand knowing that such toxicity is not my lot in life and should not be part of my day-to-day reality. If I do genuinely experience rejection or indifference, my response is no longer self-belittling. I recognize that other people's behavior toward me is not a reflection of my identity as the royal and redeemed offspring of God.

Breakthrough

We each have about five major pain cycles that play out in our day-to-day behaviors. Identifying these cycles and establishing new "thought highways" in our brains takes time and diligent effort, but it *is* possible to shift from unproductive "default" patterns to new patterns of belief, and glowing confidence is the result. When our eyes are opened and our pain cycles are broken, we experience genuine transformation from the inside out and truly come into being. Such breakthroughs of enlightenment are significant for all of us, but for those who've lived large portions of their lives disconnected from their true identity and personhood, these revelations are especially life-changing.

Steps

It's important to note that it's not *always* necessary to take an introspective trip down memory lane to reprogram negative thought patterns; this can be done just as effectively by determined, meditative acts of repetition. But for results that last, I heartily encourage you to follow the suggestions below as you work to replace your own negative core beliefs with positive patterns of response. These steps are by no means a one-size-fits-all remedy for every issue and struggle, but they are at least a good place to start:

1. Identify unhealthy, negative, or demeaning communication (either with yourself or with others). 2. Observe your physical feelings of response (such as anxiety or shakiness) when in uncomfortable or "triggering" situations. 3. Identify your emotions (such as anger, despair, sadness, jealousy, insecurity, fear, etc.) when in uncomfortable situations. 4. Trace your negative thought and behavior patterns back to their core belief (often formed in childhood or during traumatizing experiences). 5. Re-run history like a movie in your mind's eye to

forgive and release the past. 6. "Write" an appropriate new core belief on your heart such as "I am wanted," "I am lovable," "I am enough." 7. Solidify and actualize your new core beliefs through repetition and application until they become your "new normal."

Get a Grip

To lift up our voices with confidence, we must possess our own souls and live out of the true essence of who we really are. To "possess our own souls" means to take responsibility for our thoughts and emotions and the out-workings of our beliefs. This is not something that anyone can do for us. It is our personal prerogative to take responsibility for our own being and the maintenance of our connection and alignment with our divine life Source. It bears repeating that Colossians 2:10 (NASB) says, "In him you have been made complete." The word *complete* in the original Greek means, "furnished, supplied, perfected, and made replete." Our beliefs, thoughts, emotions, and actions can be established in this phenomenal completion that's already been accomplished for us through redemption. Arising into a place of wholeness is possible. The way has been made. We don't need emotional "fillers." The old cycles of pain *can* be broken. Authentic peace, joy, and vitality can be our daily experience.

Insecurity and unbelief manifest when we don't walk confidently in our redeemed state of "enough." Our self-confidence begins to crack when we doubt our worth and lovability. In emotionally unstable moments, we can tend to focus on our *apparent* lack as opposed to our already established completeness. If we yield further to this sense of inadequacy, our inner and outer dialogue will begin to negate the reality of our abundant life in God. It's a downward spiral that can get out of control all too quickly. The fact is, in and of our "earthsuit" selves, we're not adequate for the mighty calling to which we've been assigned, yet redemption has restored us to everything we need. Second Corinthians 3:5–6 (NASB) says, "Not that we are adequate in ourselves to consider anything as coming from ourselves, but our adequacy is from God, who also made us adequate." We need to get a grip on our adequacy in God. We need to boldly own it!

In the book of Philippians, Paul the apostle listed several reasons why he might have confidence in his flesh: "Circumcised on the eighth day, of the people of Israel, of the tribe of Benjamin, a Hebrew of Hebrews, as for righteousness based on the law, faultless" (Philippians 3:5–6, NIV). Despite the greatness of his heritage, Paul said, "everything is worthless when compared with the infinite value of knowing Christ Jesus" (Philippians 3:8, NLT). Like Paul, we also can take hold of the confidence that comes from knowing we're blessed, empowered, sealed, anointed, appointed, and made adequate, both now and for all eternity. Effectively lifting up our voices depends on it.

Small Saul

Saul, the first appointed king of Israel, was a man who suffered from a lack of confidence. He was handsome in appearance and imposing in stature. Physically speaking, he had every good reason to lead his nation with confidence, but his personal insecurities and fragile self-esteem caused him to make some poor decisions—decisions that ultimately cost him the crown.

Shortly after Saul was sworn in as Israel's monarch, Israel went to war with the Amalekites. Through God's prophet, Samuel, the new king was given instructions that would enable him to win the victory for Israel. This included a harsh but necessary directive to kill all the Amalekite animals. Saul, however, failed to follow through; he spared the Amalekite's best sheep and cattle. When confronted by Samuel, Saul was defensive about his actions but later confessed, "I feared the people and obeyed their voice" (1 Samuel 15:24, ESV). "I was afraid of the people and so I gave into them" (1 Samuel 15:24, NIV).

Something caused Saul to refrain from confidently lifting up his voice as the nation's leader. The clue to Saul's man-fearing, people-pleasing insecurities is found in 1 Samuel 15:17 where he's referred to as being "small in his own eyes." When we're small in our own eyes, we carry within us a void of confidence. We struggle to believe that we've got what it takes to competently fulfill our calling and adequately handle our assignments. A perception of personal lack like this debilitates us on every level.

Responsibility

When our energy is focused on compensating for our perceived inadequacies, we're hindered from arising in our potential. Saul's disobedience was a bigger deal than he realized. He not only failed to follow specific instructions, but he also gave himself over to the persuasion of other voices. These actions were highly irresponsible and placed Israel at great risk. The nation's welfare depended on its leader's willingness to hear and obey divine counsel.

Samuel was familiar with Saul's insecurity issues, but as far as consequences were concerned, Saul received little comfort for his disobedience. God is not a hard taskmaster; when he appoints us he also anoints us for everything that will be required of us. If we're given a purpose, it's up to us to trust that everything we need to fulfill that purpose will be provided. The grace of God toward us is unending, but that grace is not a compensation for our excuses. It's our God-given responsibility to take up our calling obediently and with confidence. We must not allow the vociferous and deceptive voice of our own insecurities to talk us out of our adequacy in Christ. We must stand firm in our convictions, lift up our voices, and refuse to give in to fear.

Good Enough

The Bible declares that we can do all things through the power of the Spirit—not some things, not a few things, but all things. I choose to believe it, but I haven't *always* walked consistently at that level of confidence. Despite an enviable professional résumé, I was plagued in my earlier years with a deep-rooted sense of inadequacy. It's an awful feeling that many of us can relate to—the sense that who we are and what we do is not good enough.

"Not good enough" is another expression for "missing the mark," which is actually the Greek terminology for the word sin. This idea of inadequacy, lack, or missing the mark is exactly what Satan enticed man to feed on in the Garden of Eden. That's why we must steadfastly replace thoughts of lack and inadequacy with the truth that we're made in God's likeness—furnished, supplied, and replete. It was during a prayer meeting in Virginia many years ago that God began a work to dismantle insecurity in me once and for all. And he did it through a simple yet profound challenge.

I was a regular attendee at New Life Church in Danville at the time. I loved it there; the people were friendly and the services were uplifting. I visited the Monday prayer meeting as often as I could, and on one particular night, instead of gathering us up in a circle as he usually did, Elder Ewing invited us to line up at the front of the church for prayer. He said he sensed God wanted to pour upon each of us a fresh anointing of the Holy Spirit. I was thrilled for the chance to receive a touch from God. Raising my three rambunctious, young boys on a tighter-than-tight budget was no small task. In addition to being their mummy and teacher, I was also their entertainment. As an introvert with an INFP personality type, this go-go-go lifestyle was a stretch for me. I longed to use my creative gifts again. In short, I felt as dry as a bone.

As the beloved man of God moved down the line to pray for us individually, an expectation stirred within me that something powerful was about to happen. I wasn't disappointed. The instant he touched my brow, I fell to the floor like a sack of potatoes under the supernatural power of God. For the next thirty minutes, wave after wave of divine glory washed over me. It was an extraordinary experience that felt so amazing it was nearly unbearable! I sensed Jesus standing over me, looking at me, wanting me to look back at him. With the eyes of my spirit, I saw his face. His fire-filled gaze met mine as his unconditional love washed over my soul. I could tell there was something he wanted to say.

One Resounding Word

Jesus spoke to me with one clear, resounding word. This word penetrated my spirit with such intensity and potency that the effects of it are still at work to this day. The word was this: "Obey!" In the speaking of that one word, I received permission, anointing, command, and challenge. I knew that whatever I was inspired by God to do from that time on, I was to confidently take it on with a wholehearted intention to obey, even if I'd never done it before. I knew in my heart with an absolute divine assurance that I was (and would be) fully equipped with creative power to handle every task put before me.

The word God spoke to me that day is something he's speaking to all of us. He's calling us to trust him without hesitation. The time has passed for self-doubt and over analysis. Our insecurities must not govern our actions. Once we're on our way to being healed, restored, and strengthened, we must arise in confidence and lift up our voices with boldness. "Whatever he tells you to do, do it" (John 2:5, WNT).

Do It Scared

The Bible repeatedly admonishes us to not be afraid. But that doesn't mean we won't feel scared or nervous at times, especially if we're tackling something unfamiliar. This exhortation is given to remind us that *regardless* of our emotions and feelings, we need to obey God's call (communicated to our souls through divine inspiration, hunches, and godly inclination), even if we have to do it scared! From the time the word *obey* entered my spirit as a prophetic command, I started to do things I'd never done before. I began to write books, musicals, and poetry. I began to teach and preach in conferences all over the world. Statements such as, "I don't think I can do that" or "I've never done that before" departed from my everyday vocabulary. I realized those things didn't matter anymore and had nothing to do with following divine inspiration.

God had given me a charge to obey. It was my responsibility to do just that. When it came to things that didn't come easily, comfortably, or experientially to me, I was to draw from the creative power within me to figure out how to fill in the blanks. One time, I was inspired to build a screened-in patio for my home in Richmond, Virginia. Though completely inexperienced as a carpenter, I set to task believing I could pull it off. I custom designed and built the screened area to keep the mosquitoes away, but also to inspire my three sons. I wanted them to see that if their mother could accomplish a challenging project by figuring it out as she went along, surely they could do whatever they put their minds to as well. The end result was beautiful, and we enjoyed many happy, mosquito-free hours in our new space. I spent a total of $500 and many hours of labor, but the addition added $5,000 to the value of the house.

Prepare, Listen, Obey

As we saw from the life of King Saul, communicating with strength and confidence is closely connected to recognizing and heeding spiritual inspiration. The story of Esther is a magnificent example of someone who followed divinely inspired instructions. She was simply willing to listen, obey, and lift up her voice. In doing so, she said the right thing to the right people in the right place at the right time. As a result, her nation was saved.

The story of Esther begins with King Ahasuerus of Persia holding a great feast for all the princes, nobles, and servants in his kingdom. Toward the end of the feast, King Ahasuerus called for Vashti, his queen, to come and display her beauty for all the guests to behold, but Vashti refused her husband's request. The king was humiliated and furious. In his anger, he banished Vashti from the kingdom and sent out a decree to find a new queen.

The fairest of maidens from all over Persia were gathered to the palace and given into the charge of Hegai, the king's chamberlain. There, under Hegai's care, the women received everything they needed for twelve months of beautification in preparation for the day when they would be brought before King Ahasuerus. The maiden most pleasing to the king would become his new bride and queen.

Guiding Voice

This story keenly parallels the relationship between Christ and his bride. We too are undergoing an inner beautification process to prepare us for our heavenly bridegroom. Through her careful preparation, Esther taught us an important lesson: In order to be pleasing to King Ahasuerus, she did only as Hegai, the king's extended voice of authority, advised. She wisely ascertained that Hegai knew what the king loved—that he understood what it took to obtain the king's favor. Esther was smart enough to follow Hegai's guidance. The result was this: "The king loved Esther above all the women, and she obtained grace and favor in his sight" (Esther 2:17, KJV).

We also have been given an advisor—a guide—a voice by which to be inspired and led. It is King Jesus's extended voice of authority on earth—the Holy Spirit. As we follow the Holy Spirit's guidance and inspiration, we too will experience favor and blessings with God and with man.

Not long after Esther became the new queen, great danger arose for her people, the Jews. Haman, a wicked man with a greed for power, had been appointed to a position of governmental authority. In a harsh, anti-Semitic political move completely outside of Esther's control, Haman commanded the annihilation of all the Jews in the land. Esther, urged by her relative Mordecai, agreed to appeal to King Ahasuerus for his mercy and help. But before she went to the king, she called upon her people to pray and fast. She knew if her words were to be effective, her preparation would need to be bathed in prayer and guided by divine wisdom; she understood where her help came from.

Timing Is Everything

After three days, Esther readied herself to visit the king. She understood that by entering the king's court without invitation, she was subject to the death penalty. Once again, Esther's careful preparations to captivate the king's heart did not go to waste. When she boldly entered the palace and stood before him, he was stirred by the sight of the woman he loved. Without hesitation, he chose to spare her life.

Despite the urgent plight of the Jewish people, Esther was not hasty to plead to the king for help. Instead, she exercised patience by inviting the king and Haman to a specially prepared banquet. In this way, she was letting her king know that he was first in her heart. She was demonstrating that she wasn't just out to get something from him. It was a divinely inspired action that moved the king to extend even greater favor toward his beloved queen. "The king's heart is like a stream of water directed by the Lord; he guides it wherever he pleases" (Proverbs 21:1, NLT).

At the conclusion of the feast, when the time was right for Esther to lift up her voice in appeal to the king, she knew she had his ear, his heart, *and* his stomach! Timing and divinely inspired strategy are everything. The king immediately responded to Esther's appeal by giving permission for all Jews to defend themselves and their property. Haman was exposed for being a power-hungry murderer and was sentenced to death by hanging.

The success of Esther's efforts to save her people was largely due to the confidence built within her from listening to Hegai, the king's extended voice of authority. At "such a time as this," she yielded to the wisdom of divine inspiration, lifted up her voice, and effectively executed her divinely ordained responsibilities.

Divine Inspiration

Ezekiel was another spokesman for God who understood the power of inspired obedience. In the book of Ezekiel, chapter 37, he was called to prophesy to a valley of dry bones. The bones represented the whole house of Israel. At the hearing of God's word prophesied through Ezekiel, the bones came together and sinew and flesh grew back on the bones. The Hebrew meaning of the word *prophesy* in this text is, "to speak or sing by inspiration." This is especially noteworthy considering what transpired next.

The flesh and bones came together, but there was no breath in them by which they could live. God said to Ezekiel, "Prophesy to the breath, prophesy, son of man, and say to the breath, 'Thus says the Lord God, 'Come from the four winds, O breath, and breathe on these slain, that they may come to life'" (Ezekiel 37:9 NAS). The word "breath" here in Hebrew is *ruwach*, which means "expression, function, courage, spirit, and life." Ezekiel, inspired *by* the ruwach of God, spoke *to* the ruwach of God, and partnered *with* the ruwach of God to bring to life that which was lifeless. As Ezekiel lifted up his voice with confidence, the life force of God filled the whole house of Israel. "And they came to life and stood on their feet, an exceedingly great army" (Ezekiel 37:10, NAS).

Speak Life

The mission and mandate of God's spokespeople has never changed. We're called to partner with God to release function and vitality into the "dry bones" all around us. We're called to speak life to the lifeless, hope to the hopeless, and courage to the faint of heart. When we speak, pray, and prophesy under the inspiration of the Holy Spirit, our words mold, strengthen, empower, comfort, encourage, and heal. As we align our words and actions with divine inspiration, we have the potential to effect positive change in the earth.

First Corinthians 2:12 (NASB) says, "We have received... the Spirit who is from God, so that we may know the things freely given to us by God, which things we also speak." God delights to make known to us the Kingdom treasures that are ours to use and enjoy. The Spirit of God also desires for us to use our voices as creative instruments to pray those things into being so that his kingdom can come and his will be done on earth as it is in heaven. We're further encouraged, "My word, which comes from my mouth, is like the rain and snow. It will not come back to me without results. It will accomplish whatever I want and achieve whatever I send it to do" (Isaiah 55:11, GWT). Without question, we can expect to see divinely powerful results from our divinely inspired speech.

A Voice to Be Heard

When it comes to lifting up our voices, most of us are not so unfortunate as to suffer with a speech impediment, but all too many of us have, at times, been stifled in our self-expression or required to sit down, "shut up," and be quiet. When exposed to prolonged oppression, our ability for self-expression can become paralyzed. Our feelings and ideas can get buried under insecurity as well as our hopes, dreams, and desires. Fearing the backlash we may previously have experienced in speaking up and speaking out, we can become crippled into silence and "lose our voice."

Both for our personal benefit and for the well-being of others, we're being divinely urged in this hour to find our voices once again. Too many people live with a disconnection between their heart and their verbalized communication. But God is calling us to arise in confidence and speak the truth in love.

Romans 8:19 (NAS) says, "creation waits eagerly for the revealing of the sons of God." We are the Esthers and Ezekiels of our day, called to lift up our voices on behalf of those who have no voice for themselves: sex trafficking and child pornography victims, the diseased and the destitute, the homeless, the hungry, the war-torn, those without clean water, the persecuted, the unborn, the abused, endangered animals, the environment, and more. The list of critical needs goes on and on. Our voices are a God-given gift to the world. We must arise and faithfully use them.

Comfort Zone

Lifting up our voices might involve speaking into difficult situations or simply learning to say "No." It might mean conveying an important message, communicating with kindness, or speaking out for a cause. Whatever lifting up our voice means to each of us individually, there's one thing we can be sure of: it will almost certainly require us to step out of our comfort zone.

The Old Testament judge, Deborah, understood what it meant to transcend her comfort zone. Deborah is described in the book of Judges as a prophetess—a woman inspired by God—a poetess, and a seer. Her words were important; they held authoritative, creative power. Deborah fulfilled her role as a judge in Israel with obedience and excellence, yet throughout all her years in service to her nation, I doubt she ever expected to go onto the frontlines of the battlefield.

After twenty years under the dominating iron fist of Jabin, king of Canaan, the word of the Lord came to Deborah. God revealed to Deborah that the nation of Israel would be victorious in a soon coming battle with their Canaanite oppressors. She shared the information with Barak, the commander of the Israeli army. As he prepared to go to war, Barak said to Deborah, "I will go if you go with me. But if you do not go with me, I will not go." And she said, "For sure I will go with you. But the honor will not be yours" (Judges 4:8–9, NLV). In this most unusual combat story, it was Deborah who led the troops into battle. Israel did indeed win a mighty victory, and all the honor for the military success went to a woman—something that was virtually unheard of at that time in history.

Leading the army of Israel into battle may not have been in Deborah's comfort zone, but she arose in her potential, lifted up her voice in confidence, and fulfilled her calling in that season of her life. In a song of celebration, she sang these inspiring words: "Village life in Israel ceased, ceased until I, Deborah, arose, arose a mother in Israel"

(Judges 5:7, NIV). If Deborah could arise and lift up her voice in the midst of a culture where women were barely esteemed, surely we should not allow any obstacle to stand in our way either.

Not So Big

Over two decades ago, I experienced two divine visitations from God that removed my hesitation to answer the call to arise. To this day, I still carry the strong burden for humanity that was imparted into my heart during those extraordinary meetings.

The first encounter was starkly memorable. I was in England at the time, visiting my parents in their Surrey home before heading out to South Africa for my wedding. I had sat down on the floor of their basement room to pray. Unexpectedly, the presence of the Lord came strongly into the room. It was as though every square inch of space was filled with God's peace and love. It was unforgettably beautiful.

I stilled my heart to listen, and to see what would happen next. Suddenly, I saw before me the world, as if hanging in space like a globe turning slowly on its axis. It was the size of a man's fist, hovering just below eye level about fifteen inches from my body. As I beheld this vision of planet earth, I remember being struck with a distinct thought—a thought I immediately verbalized in my heart to God. "It's not so big!" I said excitedly, "*It's not so big!*" I understood that the Eternal Spirit was showing me the world from a divine perspective. He was letting me see that the world is not so big that it cannot be reached—that it's possible for *everyone* to hear the message of redeeming love.

Then something amazing happened. I felt God reach inside my chest and "open up my heart with his hands" the way one might divide a large batch of bread dough into two equal parts. Once my heart was fully opened, I saw God's hands cup around the back of the world (that still "hung" suspended before me). Slowly and gently, he pushed the world toward me and tucked it into my heart. Then, he closed my heart around the world and the vision came to a close.

What happened that day is so much more to me than a beautiful memory; it's a mandate that never leaves me. From the moment the world was placed in my heart, I have cared and prayed for its people like they're my very own children. The Savior of all mankind wants us to know: the world is ours to reach, and it's not too big.

Returning King

A second and equally unforgettable vision came to me just a few months later in Johannesburg. Again, it was an encounter that took place during a time I'd set aside for prayer. After about thirty minutes of heartfelt worship and singing songs of praise, God's glory suddenly rushed into the room. The Shekinah presence flooded the atmosphere with such intensity and strength that I was completely taken aback. It was a power so inexplicable and overwhelming, I was unable to remain upright. I fell prostrate to the floor and buried my face in the carpet. I had felt God's presence before, and have felt it many times since, but not like this. This was different. The revelation I experienced in that hour was not of God's comfort and peace; it was that of a returning King.

As I lay face down, the words of Matthew 25:6 (WE) came prominently to mind. "At midnight there was a cry, 'Behold! The bridegroom is coming! Come out to meet him!'" Though difficult to describe, I felt as though I was "living inside" the parable of the ten virgins—inside the hearts and minds of the five whose lamps were lit with oil, but most especially, the five whose lamps were not. But the context in which I was experiencing the parable was not ten girls in dresses from two thousand years ago; it was multitudes of modern day men and women devoid of, or disconnected from, God's saving light and presence within them.

I became acutely aware of the indifference many of these people had previously shown to the gospel message (not least of all because the message had been presented to them in a dogmatic, cold-hearted, and legalistic fashion). But now, as they saw the King of kings returning, I could feel their sense of unreadiness for eternity. I could feel their terrified panic inside me. It was the most grievous thing I have ever encountered. I was also aware of multitudes more who knew nothing of the reality of God's unconditional love. I could "hear" them crying out from all over the world. They wanted to find home but did not know the way.

As I heard these cries, the presence of God intensified to an even greater degree. I wanted to be buried into the floor facedown—to get as low and as prostrate as I possibly could. I felt as though I had the weight of fifty wool blankets upon my back, yet I longed to be covered still more. The holy presence around me was indescribably powerful.

Final Hour

For about two hours, I lay in this vision feeling the weight of God's glory and experiencing the anguish of unprepared hearts. Slowly, the presence of God "lifted," and eventually, I was able to sit up. I could neither speak nor eat for the rest of the day nor the day that followed. I could only weep with distress at the sight and sound of millions despairing in their final hour.

The impact of what I saw and heard during that extraordinary visitation has never left me. Though the vision took place over twenty years ago, the message it conveyed still rings true today: All over the world, there are millions of people who feel lost, disconnected, and afraid. They need to hear our voices of hope and the message of eternal love. It is time for us to align our beliefs, thoughts, communication, and actions to the clarity and positive influence that are ours in the power of God. Multitudes are longing to find their way home, and it's up to us to help them get there.

It is time to arise.

It is time to lift up your voice.

Reflections

_____

_____

_____

_____

_____

_____

_____

_____

_____

_____

_____

_____

_____

Final Word

Thank you for joining me on this powerful journey of ascension and coming into being. It is my sincere hope that you've been able to glean some useful insights along the way that will equip you to arise daily in the fullness of your potential.

It's empowering to know that the low moments in our lives can serve as pictures of contrast between dis-ease and happiness. When viewed wisely, these crucible experiences can propel us to find alignment with the peace, joy, love, and vitality that we truly desire.

As I write this final word, I'm experiencing levels of productivity and satisfaction in my daily life that, at one time, I wouldn't have considered possible. I'm living and moving and enjoying my being in congruent, intimate connection with the Source of all love and life.

It is my heartfelt prayer that you will experience this quality of arising also. I want you to know that you have the power to write the remaining chapters of your story here on earth any way you choose. These chapters will be testimonies of authentic restoration as you arise from your wounds, shake off your ashes, and grow confident in your value and worth. They will be demonstrations of joy and redemption as you walk in freedom and follow paths that immerse you in your passions and purposes.

As you put on your strength, lift up your voice, and embrace the divine identity that is yours in the likeness of God, your life will overflow with love and light, and your destiny will unfold with grace and ease. If ever there was a time to arise it's now. Can you hear the call?

It is time.

It is time to arise.

Also by Michele

Love Song

Poems of Connection

Coming 2018

About Michele

Michele Francesca Cohen was born and raised in the beautiful county of Surrey, England and is currently based out of Dallas, Texas. She is a dynamic speaker for conferences, churches, and multi-media broadcasts. With over thirty years of international stage and ministry experience, Michele is appreciated for her heart-warming authenticity, her love for people, and for effective materials that equip, enlighten, and transform. For more information and links to additional publications visit www.michelefrancesca.com.